Motivation
Strategies, theory and practice

The Authors

Professor Ivan Robertson is an occupational psychologist who has worked in industry, public service and universities. His interest in motivation reflects a general concern with the psychological factors involved in the performance and well-being of people at work. He is Associate Editor of the *British Journal of Psychology*, Co-editor of the *International Review of Industrial and Organizational Psychology* and past Chair of the North of England branch of the British Psychological Society.

Dr Mike Smith is a Senior Lecturer in industrial psychology. After graduating at Liverpool University, he worked in a research unit attached to the Department of Psychology before going to work in industry as head of a small research unit on training. On returning to a university career at the Department of Applied Psychology at University of Wales Institute of Science and Technology, Cardiff, he continued his specialization in the areas of selection and assessment, careers advice and organizational surveys. He has held the position of Honorary Secretary of the Division of Occupational Psychology of the British Psychological Society and served on a number of other bodies including the Manpower Services Commission and the University of Manchester Appointments Board.

Dominic Cooper entered higher education as a mature student after many years working in industry. He is both an occupational psychologist and ergonomist whose current research interests are concerned with the appli theories to health and safet quality improvement issues.

All three authors are in th of Management at the Univ Institute of Science and Techi

The Institute of Personnel and Development is the leading publisher of books and reports for personnel and training professionals and students and for all those concerned with the effective management and development of people at work. For full details of all our titles please telephone the Publishing Department on 0181 946 9100.

Motivation
Strategies, theory and practice

Ivan T Robertson
Mike Smith
Dominic Cooper

Second edition

Institute of Personnel and Development

© Ivan T Robertson, Mike Smith and Dominic Cooper, 1985,
1987 1992
First published 1985 as *Motivation and job design*
Reprinted 1987
Second edition, with new title and new material, 1992
Reprinted 1994

Printed in Great Britain by
The Cromwell Press, Melksham, Wiltshire

British Library Cataloguing in Publication Data

Robertson, Ivan T.
   Motivation: Strategies, Theory and
   Practice. − 2 Rev. ed
   I. Title   II. Smith, Mike
   III. Cooper, Dominic
   658.3

   ISBN 0-85292-488-7

**INSTITUTE OF PERSONNEL
AND DEVELOPMENT**

IPD House, Camp Road, London SW19 4UX
Tel: 0181 946 9100   Fax: 0181 947 2570
Registered office as above. Registered Charity No. 1038333
A company limited by guarantee. Registered in England No. 2931892

Contents

List of figures   vii
Preface   ix

1 INTRODUCTION: MOTIVATION
AND ORGANIZATIONS   1
    Socio-technical systems theory   5
    Organization structure   9
    Organization structure and technology   11
    Organizational climate   13
    The total organizational system   15
    People and organizations   16
    Psychological models, individual and
        organizational effectiveness   18

2 MOTIVATION THEORIES AND
WORK BEHAVIOUR   19
    Content and process theories   19
    Implications for managers   29
    Implications for organizations   30
    Behavioural approaches   30
    The organizational behaviour modification system   34
    Goal-setting   38
    Setting realistic goals   41
    Control theory   47
    Equity   48
    An integration   50

3 WORK CHARACTERISTICS THAT
MOTIVATE   51
    Tasks   52
    Job characteristics and motivation   56
    Task characteristics   58
    The job (task) characteristics combined   62

Socio-technical systems approaches to job design 69
Redesigning jobs 72
Job context characteristics 72

4 MEASURING MOTIVATION IN
  ORGANIZATIONS 78
    Three case studies of measuring organizational
      motivation 78
    Uses of measuring motivation in organizations 83
    Financial implications of measuring motivation 88
    Practical aspects of measuring motivation 89

5 JOB AND WORK DESIGN AS PLANNED
  CHANGE 102
    The rationale of job design 102
    Four main contextual influences on job design 103
    Different types of job enrichment 106
    Job and work design as planned change 107
    An evaluation of job design 114

6 JOB AND WORK DESIGN: SOME EXAMPLES 121
    Goal setting and job design 122
    Forms of job and work design 123
    The impact of new technology 123
    Work groups 127
    Established and greenfield sites 131
    An overview 134

7 MOTIVATION AT WORK 137
    The importance of motivation 137
    Individual differences in motivation 138
    Sex and motivation 140
    Managerial action and motivation 144
    Conclusion 172

References 174
Author index 185
Subject index 189

List of figures

1 Productivity indexes for two different production
systems in coal mining 8
2 Absence rates (per cent of possible shifts) for two
different production systems in coal mining 8
3 Subsystems within an organization 9
4 Structural dimensions of organizations 10
5 Consequences of behaviour and their effects 32
6 The relationship between goal difficulty and
performance 42
6a The relationship between subjective probability of
success and performance 42
6b The relationship between goal difficulty and subjective
probability of success 42
7 The job description 53
8 Advantages and disadvantages of nine methods of job
analysis 54
9 The job characteristics model 63
10 How to improve key job characteristics 70
11 Approaches to job design 73
12 Work-context factors related to motivation and
satisfaction 76
13 Analysis of two jobs using the job diagnostic survey
(JDS) 83
14 Graph for determining sample size 90
15 Motivators commonly surveyed 93
16 Measures of organizational characteristics often
included in surveys 95
17 Diagram of a set of satisfaction scores from the Job
Descriptive Index (JDI) 98
17a Diagram of satisfaction scores from JDI with
scores of individual departments superimposed 98
18 A systems diagram of job design 110
19 Comparison of four motivational techniques 119

20 Changes in percentages of employees involved in job rotation at Volvo's Torslanda plant   128
21 Results from a group work redesign study   130
22 Satisfaction scores for different age groups   139
23 Satisfaction scores for men and women   141
24 Satisfaction of different categories of workers   142
25 Characteristics of a motivating environment   153
26 The matrix structure of Marks and Spencer's engineering department   155
27 Organization and person factors influenced by job design   161
28 Morale curve in unemployment   166

Preface

This new edition of our earlier book *Motivation and Job Design*, is based upon the belief that scientific research has much to offer that is of the utmost importance to practical affairs in the workplace. Within recent years, occupation psychology has developed rapidly and produced considerable additional information towards understanding the psychological processes involved in motivating people at work. We have attempted to provide an easily understood and readable introduction to the underlying principles and practical applications of motivation theory for the practising manager and student alike. At times we have presented complex ideas and research evidence, but this has been done as straightforwardly as possible while avoiding over simplification. Our firm view is that good practice is based on a sound knowledge of underlying principles. Throughout the book we have assumed that our readers are interested in sturdy solutions based on firm principles, rather than a 'quick fix' approach. We hope that we have been successful in presenting our material in a balanced way.

Many recent developments have been incorporated into this book and, as well as including new material on various aspects of motivation such as goal-setting and job design, we have also applied current knowledge to the concept of Total Quality Management in an attempt to highlight solutions to various important practical problems. We are grateful to have benefitted from the exchange of ideas with colleagues at the Manchester School of Management, and would also like to thank Anne Cordwent at the Institute of Personnel Management for her encouragement and patience during the preparation of the manuscript.

ITR, JMS, MDC
1992

1 Introduction: motivation and organizations

Work is a central part of many people's lives in modern society. When asked if people would continue to work in the absence of any financial need 69 per cent of a sample of men and 65 per cent of a sample of women from the British workforce said yes (Warr 1982). Clearly this does not mean that people enjoy all aspects of work nor that people prefer work to other activities. It does however support the view that work plays an important role in life and meets significant needs that people have. Warr (1982) has reviewed the functions that work fulfils for people and identifies the following benefits of having a job:

money
activity
variety
temporal structure
social contacts
status and identity in society.

The most obvious benefit of a job is that it provides income for the job holder. Although the importance of this benefit should not be understated, it is clear from the percentage of people who would continue to work if they did not need the money that there is more to work than financial gain. The activity provided by a job gives people an opportunity to use their skills and knowledge. A job provides variety by taking people out of their domestic environment and for most people a job also influences the way their time is structured and used. The social aspects of work include an opportunity and an environment in which to interact with others and the provision of status and identity within society. In our society for example the question 'What do you do?' has only one meaning, 'What *work* do you do?'.

This book is concerned not merely with work, but with the related concepts of motivation and work. Motivation is a psychological concept related to the *strength* and *direction* of human behaviour. For example, problems such as why two people with the same ability produce different levels of performance, or why someone works hard at one task but shirks another, may be explained in terms of motivation. The bulk of this book deals with theories, research evidence and practical issues that relate to motivation and work behaviour. This chapter is designed to set the scene for the remaining chapters and is concerned with the context in which work is conducted. For most people work takes place within an organization and modern organizations include large multinational corporations, public service organizations, small firms of 20 or so people and a host of other possibilities. It is important therefore to examine the nature of organizations and some of the relationships that exist between the characteristics of organizations and work behaviour.

Early approaches towards improving work performance within organizational contexts were characterized by an emphasis on instrumentality, which is the use of work as a tool to attain various ends such as output.

The emphasis on instrumentality has many sources. Ellul (1964) traces its origin to the second half of the nineteenth century when there occurred the 'absorption, to a greater and greater extent, of the entire man in the economic network' and the devaluation of all human activities and tendencies other than the economic. Thence arose the validation of the producing-consuming part of man, while all his other facets were gradually erased. Another source lay in the rising problems of labour management at the turn of the nineteenth century, occasioned particularly by the rise of trade unionism. Scientific management was intended by its creator, F W Taylor, to be a rational solution to the industrial uncertainties of that period which would benefit both employers and workers. But:

. . . employers looked upon scientific management exactly as Taylor has insisted that they should not: as an arsenal of devices designed to simplify and improve the management of labour. They might adopt the piecework and bonus system, but neglect time-and-motion studies. They might conduct such studies, but neglect Taylor's ideas on foremanship (Bendix, 1956).

This selective approach to scientific management, stemming from the desire for a more efficient control of labour, laid the basis for a mechanistic rationalization of work which reached its most sophisticated expression in the theory and practice of industrial engineering.

Yet another source of instrumentality was the need to minimize production costs, especially in the increasingly competitive markets which characterized many mass-production industries. In a United States survey published in 1955, it was found that the criteria used in the design of industrial jobs were based largely on a principle of 'minimum cost'. The three major criteria were: maximum specialization through the limitation of both the number of component tasks in a job and variations in tasks; maximum repetitiveness and minimum training time.

The distinctiveness of instrumentality lies in its assumptions, firstly that a rationalized emasculation of work is the best or only way of achieving goals of high output and low cost and, secondly, that work has no outcomes other than economic ones. This view must be understood as a product of its time.

Current views of work are more inclusive. We have, in the first place, a developing theoretical knowledge about people at work produced by behavioural sciences, as well as a more informed approach to the general problem of managing organizations. In addition, wider social changes are significantly modifying the ways in which we view work and organizations.

In a review of organization theories Veen (1984) identifies four traditional approaches: scientific management (Taylor, 1911), the bureaucratic approach of Weber (1947), (Mayo 1951) the scientific administration approach (Gulick and Urwick, 1937) and the human relations school (Roethlisberger and Dickson, 1939; Mayo, 1945).

Like Taylor's scientific management each of these approaches were products of their time. Weber's work argued that organizations designed in accordance with certain key bureaucratic principles would, from a purely technical point of view, be 'capable of attaining the highest degree of

3

efficiency and is in this sense formally the most rational known means of carrying out imperative control over human beings' (Weber 1947, p 337). Other authors have shown however that there are flaws in the bureaucratic model (Merton, 1957; Gouldner 1954).

Veen (1984) summarizes the four approaches as follows:

The four classical approaches put forward a number of problems which the organization must solve, and for which the approaches propose what is in principle a solution:

The *scientific management* approach emphasizes the problem of how the individuals' working capacity can be utilized in the most efficient way possible, and how people can themselves be allowed to reap the benefits of this efficiency. The solution for this problem is sought in maximalization of the structuring and instrumentalization of the task, and in remuneration for work done.

The bureaucratic approach puts forward the problem of how the organization can be protected against internal and external disturbances. Control and coordination of organizational operations is realized by means of a hierarchical structure and a system of rules.

The *scientific administration* approach consists primarily of a pragmatic development of the bureaucratic idea, and gives directions for how to manage an organization efficiently. As in the bureaucratic approach, the emphasis lies upon internal efficiency.

The *human relations* approach directs its attention to how the needs of people can be reconciled with organizational goals. . . .

The different approaches demonstrate that the organization must navigate among a number of reefs to arrive at a solution for this problem. It must control the behaviour of its members, and steer it in the direction most favourable for the organization as a whole, but must at the same time take care that these individuals remain sufficiently motivated. (Veen, 1984, p 720–1).

Each traditional approach looks at organizations from a different perspective and emphasizes different issues. Economic affluence has led to a diminished concern with satisfying basic

4

needs, while improvements in the extent and quality of education, along with the erosion of traditional patterns of authority, are leading people to think increasingly in terms of satisfying their higher-order needs, particularly those of self-actualization and self-determination. As a result, we are beginning to ask much more from our organizations; instead of simply serving them, we want to know how they can contribute to the quality of our work experience and personal development. All these movements have resulted in a shift of emphasis from the extrinsic rewards of work to its intrinsic rewards.

Overall, these changes have compelled us to look at jobs from the viewpoint of the employee as well as that of the organization. While earlier approaches to job design implied a technologically-determined view of human behaviour at work, current views state that behaviour is a *joint product of technological and social (human) factors*. From this it follows that optimal performance results only from the reciprocal integration of the technological and human aspects of the job. The interdependent nature of the person-technology relationship is brought out more clearly in the definition of job design as the 'specification of the contents, the methods and the relationships of jobs to satisfy the requirement of the technology and organization as well as the social and personal requirements of the job holder.' (Davis, 1966).

In other words, modern organizational life is a complex interplay of various elements within a very complex total system.

Socio-technical systems theory

Socio-technical systems theory represents an explicit attempt by organization specialists to develop an understanding of organizations that embodies social and technological factors. The socio-technical approach to organizations was developed during the 1950s by a group of researchers at the Tavistock Institute in England. In its simplest form the socio-technical systems approach attempts to identify and understand the interactions that take place between the social and technological elements of organizations. An early (now classic) example of the work of the Tavistock socio-technical systems researchers is given in the work of Trist and his colleagues (1951) in the British coal-mining industry. Their work demonstrates how the socio-technical systems approach can be used to understand and then influence organizational factors. The traditional method of coal getting (the short wall method) involved small groups of miners, usually two or three, working closely together. These groups enjoyed a high level of discretion, in that control over the task was wholly internal to the group (miners even chose their own work-mates), and the only contact the group had with external colliery management was in contracting to work a particular wall of the coal face. Within these small undifferentiated groups each coal miner was called on to execute a variety of tasks, often substituting for his mate. In addition, group members experienced a sense of contribution inasmuch as they completed the entire cycle of operations necessary to hew a given face.

The technological innovation consisted of substituting mechanical coal-cutters and conveyors for the old hand-got methods, thus transforming the production technology to a type characteristic of mass production methods. Instead of working a series of short faces, a costly method of coal extraction, mechanization made it possible to work a single long wall. The new long wall method demanded a different form of individual and group working than prevailed with the hand-got method. The production unit was organized around the cycle group of about 40 men who had to extract about 200 tons of coal per cycle. A cycle extended over 24 hours, made up of three shifts of 7½ hours each. The allocation of workmen to each shift was approximately 10 to the first 'cutting' shift, 10 to the second 'ripping' shift, and 20 to the third 'filling' shift. Within each of the shifts, individuals were restricted to narrowly defined work roles in contrast to the task variety inherent in the hand-got method. However, the real lack of integration between the miners and the technology lay in the high degree of interdependence between the tasks throughout the entire cycle. Operational problems experienced at one stage of the process were carried forward to later stages and because the inflexible nature of the production process did not permit the carrying on of later tasks while hold-ups were being dealt with, the system was necessarily highly sensitive to disruption both at the production and

6

social-psychological levels. Moreover, since discretion was no longer functionally vested in the working group, the miners experienced a sense of impotence and frustration in the face of the complex and inflexible technological system. Consequently they developed various defensive manoeuvres: a norm of low productivity as a means of reducing disturbances which were beyond their control; the creation of small informal groups whose major obligations were to themselves and not to the cycle system as a whole; individual competition for the more workable parts of the coal face and for special favours from co-workers whose own work could help or hinder one's particular task area. Absenteeism, as a means of withdrawal, also became widespread.

In a later series of studies in other coalfields, the Tavistock researchers were able to compare the efficiency of the conventional long wall method of extraction with another method, the composite long wall method, which, while still employing the new technology described above, utilized some of the design features of the older manual methods, especially discretion for means and skill. In the composite method, men arriving for a new shift take up the cycle point left by the previous shift. When their main task is completed, they then carry on with the next task, whether or not this happens to be part of the current cycle or begins another cycle. That is, unlike the men in conventional long walling, they act somewhat independently of the strict cycle process determined by the technology. The composite method also provides a greater variety of skills for the individual worker, thus making for greater job satisfaction. Composite teams are also self-selected and are paid on a common pay rate in which all group members share equally. Figures 1 and 2 (page 8) show the relative efficiency levels of teams working the same technology and coal seam but with different job designs.

The socio-technical systems approach emphasizes the interaction between human and technological factors, and modern 'open-systems' theories of organizations (eg Katz and Kahn, 1978) attempt to deal with all of the various systems and subsystems that interact to constitute an organization. A system has been defined as 'A set of interrelated elements, each of which is related directly or indirectly to every other element, and no subset of which is unrelated to every other element.' (Ackoff and Emery, 1972).

7

Figure 1

Figure 1
Productivity indexes for two different
production systems in coal mining

Index	Long wall	
	Conventional	Composite
Productivity (% of coal face potential)	78	95
State of cycle progress:		
In advance	0	22
Normal	31	73
Behind	69	5

Figure 2
Absence rates (per cent of possible shifts) for
two different production systems in
coal mining

Reasons for absence	Long wall	
	Conventional	Composite
No reason given	4.3	0.4
Sickness and other	8.9	4.6
Accident	6.8	3.2
Total	20.0	8.2

In its simplest form an open system involves an input, a transformation process and an output. Thus, viewing an organization as an open system involves examining the inputs to the organization, what the organization does with these inputs and finally the outputs or products/services of the organization.

The open-systems approach to organizations emphasizes that an organization is, in turn, composed of many different subsystems, for example the technology, the social system, the formal system (rules, regulations etc).

There are many possible systems or subsystems that need to be considered when one is trying to understand and produce a comprehensive model of an organization. Some of the major factors are shown in figure 3. In practice, each of the sub-systems of organizations can be isolated and studied, to some extent, separately.

Figure 3
Subsystems within an organization

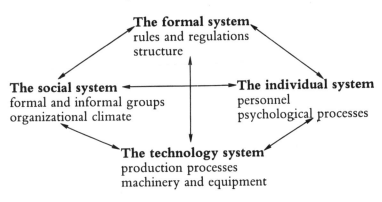

The major interest in motivation is concerned with individual and group behaviour and the remaining chapters of the book focus on these particular subsystems. It is important however to remember that these subsystems are part of a much larger interacting set of subsystems (as Ackoff and Emery's definition emphasizes). The important aspects of organizations that provide the context for individual/group motivation and performance are:

    structure
    technology
    culture/climate.

Organization structure

Structure is important to organizations to the extent that different structures may be more or less effective as far as the organization's goals are concerned. The major dimensions of organization structure relate to factors such as the number of levels in the organization's hierarchy, the extent to which control is centralized, the spans of control of managers and supervisors. Although there is not total agreement there are various structural characteristics that most organization

9

theorists would recognize as important. In a long and influential programme of research Pugh and colleagues (eg Pugh and Hickson, 1976) have studied the major dimensions of organization structure and identified the underlying factors that seem to underpin these dimensions (see figure 4). Other researchers (eg James and Jones, 1976) have proposed similar sets of dimensions.

Figure 4
Structural dimensions of organizations
(after Pugh and Hickson, 1976)

SPECIALIZATION
The extent to which specialized tasks and roles are allocated to members

STANDARDIZATION
The extent to which an organization has standard procedures

FORMALIZATION
The degree to which rules, procedures, instruction etc are written down

CENTRALIZATION
The degree to which certain aspects of authority and decision-making are located at the top of the organization's hierarchy

CONFIGURATION
The shape of the organization's role structure (eg whether there are many or few levels of authority)

As far as organization structure is concerned it has been argued (eg Handy, 1976) that a good structure will need to take account of two somewhat conflicting requirements: *uniformity* and *diversity*. On the one hand pressures for uniformity can include: the cheapness of standardization, ie it costs less to produce and process standard forms and training for standard procedures is less costly; the need for interchangeability, ie operations such as those conducted by banks, airlines or postal services often require common procedures so that information and work can be exchanged. Other pressures for uniformity identified by Handy (1976) are the need for control of the process, the need for a standard product, the need for specialization and the desire for central control.

On the other hand organizations experience pressures for

diversity which can include: goal diversity, eg the goal of the sales manager may be for high turnover, while the production manager may be aiming to keep costs as low as possible (see Lorsch *et al*, 1978). Other pressures for diversity identified by Handy (1976) include regional (geographical) diversity, market diversity, product diversity, technological diversity.

A major dilemma for many organizations concerns the balance between the need for task-division and coordination. To function many organizations need to divide the tasks to be conducted between divisions, units, departments and individual people. This division of tasks brings with it a need for the work of separate sections and people to be coordinated. Successful organizations need to develop structures that can cope with these needs.

Organization structure and technology

At one stage in the development of organization theory the notion that there might be a single 'best' design for organization structure was popular. Various systematic pieces of research demonstrated however that different structures are needed in different circumstances. Woodward (1958) for example showed that different structural factors, eg span of control, were linked to the type of production processes, eg technology, used in organizations. The structure of successful organizations within each type of production process differed from the structures of successful organizations using other production processes. Other research (eg Lawrence and Lorsch, 1967; Burns and Stalker, 1961) has shown that organization design can be linked with wider environmental factors such as the consumer market or rates of technological change.

It is also clear that there are complex interrelationships between factors such as technology and structure (Bedeian, 1980) and between these characteristics of organizations and individual employees' perceptions, motivation and behaviour (Payne and Pugh, 1976; Mansfield, 1984). The relationships are complex and it is difficult to establish clear trends. Individual motivation, attitudes and behaviour are likely to be much more directly and powerfully affected by the detailed design and nature of jobs people do than by macro organizational characteristics (see Oldham and Hackman, 1981). The in-

11

fluence of jobs and tasks on motivation is explored fully in chapter 3.

The research of people such as Woodward (1958, 1965), Burns and Stalker (1961) and Lawrence and Lorsch (1967) makes it clear that there is no such thing as a 'best', single design for organizations. The form of organization that is most appropriate depends on a variety of factors. Lawrence and Lorsch (1969) used the term *contingency* to describe the concept involved. Contingency theory makes use of some complex ideas concerning the interrelationships between organizational variables. Two of the most important concepts are those of *congruence* and *determinism*. Congruence refers to the extent to which two factors are well-matched. For example, the structure of an organization needs to be appropriate for the technology that the organization uses. Congruence is achieved when there is a good 'fit' between the technology used and the structure of the organization. Congruence between the organization's structure and the economic and social environment is also needed; the work of Burns and Stalker (1961) for instance suggests that a very formal, bureaucratic organization with rigid rules and regulations would not be congruent with a rapidly changing technologically-based market determined by contextual factors. In brief, contingency theory proposes that an effective and efficient organization needs to achieve congruence between various factors. Determinism takes this view a stage further and argues that various organizational characteristics (eg structure) are actually caused or determined by contextual factors.

Many details of the contingency theory have been questioned and challenged but few people would quarrel with the basic premise that congruence is a useful concept and that a high degree of congruence is linked with an organization's efficiency and effectiveness. Problems begin to arise however when questions such as what is meant by effectiveness or efficiency are raised.

The ideas and research conducted within a contingency theory framework and the recognition of the many complex and sometimes competing forces operating within organizations make it difficult to develop prescriptions for organizational effectiveness. When discussing organizational effectiveness Pfeffer (1978) notes that '. . . the critical question becomes not how organizations should be designed to maximize effectiveness, but rather, whose preferences and interests are to be served by the organization' (p 223). A century ago there may have been little debate on such a question; now, with increased emphasis on improving the quality of work-life and designing work to take human, as well as technical considerations, into account, questions of this nature underlie the apparently straightforward notions of organizational effectiveness.

Another problem with the notion of efficiency or effectiveness at the organizational level is that a clear idea of effectiveness requires a clear idea of the goals or aims of the organization. Research has shown fairly clearly that in many organizations goals are not shared and accepted by all members of an organization and indeed contradictory goals are sometimes pursued simultaneously or successively within an organization (see Cyert and March, 1963, Lorsch et al, 1978).

Organizational climate

Managers and other members of an organization may, by virtue of their day to day actions, create an atmosphere that is sometimes referred to as managerial climate (McGregor, 1960). Organizational climate is a broader concept than managerial climate and is influenced by factors such as the goals and aims of the organization, management practices, organization structure, degree of individual autonomy, warmth and support received from others in the organization (see Campbell et al, 1970, Payne and Pugh, 1976).

The general idea that each organization has its own climate is easy to accept and grasp. The formal definition and measurement of climate is, however, much more troublesome. Many researchers emphasize that organizational climate has a subjective property. In other words, to some extent, whatever climate an individual employee perceives him or herself to be in is the crucial factor. Indeed it seems self evident that the climate of the organization is in part a subjective and personal phenomenon. On the other hand it seems equally clear that some aspects of 'objective' reality (eg the organization's structure) will help to determine climate. Various proposals have been put forward to resolve this problem and there is now general acceptance that the organization climate is a function of both the individual person

13

and the organization and depends on the interaction between the two (James *et al*, 1978).

James and Jones (1974) go further than this and distinguish between *psychological climate*, an individual attribute and *organizational climate*, a situational attribute. James *et al* (1978) provide further clarification of the climate concept and stress that psychological climate is:

the individual's cognitive representations of relatively proximal situational conditions, expressed in terms that reflect psychologically meaningful interpretations of the situation. (p 786).

What this seems to mean is that psychological climate represents the views that people develop of the situation that they work in. James *et al* (1978) emphasize two other points. First that individuals are influenced by *their own* perceptions of the situation and not by the situation *per se*; and, as a consequence of this, '. . . individuals with different experiences and synthesizing capabilities may have different cognitive schemes and thus different perceptions of the same situation' (p 805). In other words different people in the same situation (organization) may experience different psychological climates.

As far as the measurement of climate is concerned James *et al* note that with few exceptions existing measures of climate are designed to measure situational attributes (ie organizational climate) not psychological climate. They suggest some questionnaires that may be better than others for the purposes of measuring psychological climate but conclude that, as yet, there is no single acceptable measuring instrument. Measurements of factors such as organizational climate are discussed in more detail in chapter 4. From the point of view of current theory and research this work is important and interesting. From a more practical and pragmatic perspective the distinctions may be less crucial. The important point here is that various aspects of climate are related to organizational characteristics (such as structure and technology) and to individual attitudes and behaviour (see Rousseau, 1978, Sutton and Rousseau, 1979 and Jones and James, 1979). Despite these and other studies the problem with current climate research and theory is that it is not possible to discern clear general trends and guidelines. Thus we are left with a factor that appears to play an important role in determining motivation, performance and satisfaction – but the role is unclear. Fortunately, although the influences of overall climate are not clear the links between many of the factors that determine climate: motivation, performance and satisfaction are better elaborated and understood (eg individual psychological processes, the tasks that people conduct, management practices, rewards and goals) and at various points in this book discussion focuses on these factors.

The total organizational system

Figure 3 presents some of the main systems that constitute modern organizations and one of the main contributions of this open-systems theory is that it points to the fact that organizations are made up of interrelated subsystems *and* that organizations may be examined at different levels of analysis, eg the total organization, the group and the individual person. A completely comprehensive systems model of an organization is clearly an impossibility but various models have been proposed that encompass the major systems involved in organizations and show how they interact. One such approach which provides a useful overall view of the components of an organization has been developed by Kotter (1978). Kotter's system involves the following major components:

1 *Key organizational processes:* the major information-gathering, communication, decision-making, matter/energy transporting and matter/energy converting actions of the organization's employees and machines.

2 *External environment:* an organization's task environment includes suppliers (of labour, information, materials and so on), markets, competitors and other factors related to the organization's current products and services. The wider environment includes factors such as public attitudes, the economic and political systems, laws, etc.

3 *Employees and other tangible assets:* employees, plant and office equipment, tools etc.

4 *Formal organizational arrangements:* formal systems explicitly designed to regulate the actions of employees (and machines).

5 *The social system:* including values and norms shared by employees and structure (ie relationships between em-

15

ployees in terms of such variables as power, affiliation and trust).

6 *Technology:* the major techniques that are used by employees while engaging in organizational processes and that are programmed into an organization's machines.

7 *The dominant coalition:* the objectives and strategies, the personal characteristics and the internal relationships of that minimum group of co-operating employees who oversee the organization as a whole and control its basic policymaking.

It would be wrong to infer from the static list of organizational components that various characteristics of organizations (even structural ones) are stable and unchanging. Various authors (eg Weick, 1979) stress that members of organizations are continually influencing and changing organizational characteristics.

People and organizations

As Weick (1979) and other authors make clear, people are influenced by and in turn exert an influence on the organizations in which they work. To function in any way at all organizations need to have certain functions in order to coordinate and manage the work of members of the organization. It is in the exercise of these functions that much of the interaction between people and organizations takes place. Many authors have put forward proposals on the essential functions that are involved in managing people's behaviour in organizational settings.

Gulick (1937), for example, identified seven functions:

1 planning
2 organizing
3 staffing
4 directing
5 coordinating
6 reporting
7 budgeting.

Other authors, concerned with the management and control of information systems, suggest slightly different components. Regardless of differences in emphasis and slightly different functions proposed by different authors it is clear that the management of organizations does require a number of key functions. After a review of the available literature Bagchus and van Dooren (1984) identify four common functions: planning, organizing, directing and controlling.

Planning means establishing objectives. Organizing is required to ensure that the work needed to achieve the objectives is carried out. Directing is necessary to stimulate the members of the organization into achieving the objectives. In the controlling phase the results actually achieved are compared with the objectives. A discussion of the content of these four functions gives some idea – albeit at a relatively high level of abstraction – of the total management task that must be carried out within the organization. (p 862).

The exercise of these functions has enormous influence on people who work in organizations and the effective management of these functions within an organization requires a good grasp of human psychological characteristics.

As all practising managers realize planning, organizing, controlling and directing the behaviour of other human beings are highly skilled activities. When these organizational functions are managed inefficiently a multitude of problems may arise.

Some organizational psychologists will go further than this and argue that the mere exercise of some of these functions (regardless of how skilfully they are conducted) can lead to certain forms of dysfunctional behaviour amongst employees within organizations. For example, it is suggested that control systems in themselves may lead to dysfunctional behaviour (Lawler, 1976; Lawler and Rhode, 1976). For example, people may react to control systems by developing rigid, bureaucratic modes of behaviour or even by directly opposing the control system. Bagchus and van Dooren (1984) quote an example of rigid bureaucratic behaviour first described by Blau (1955):

Civil servants at an employment bureau had the job of acting as employment agency between companies and job-hunters. Management used certain statistical data (eg the number of interviews with job-hunters per civil

17

servant) as control of their task performance. The result was that they tried to conduct as many interviews as possible, which led to wasting time and neglecting their real task as intermediary. (p 875).

Argyris (1974; see Leavitt, Pondy and Boje, 1980) has argued that there is a basic conflict between human psychological growth and human needs and the requirements of organizations. He argues that the psychological development of people is towards becoming autonomous and independent individuals who exercise control over their own world. Organizations, particularly those with a more bureaucratic and formal structure, require that people behave in a dependent fashion, follow orders and submit to external control. Thus in some organizations there is a lack of congruence between individual urges for growth and the needs of the organization (see Argyris, p 226, in Leavitt, Pondy and Boje).

Psychological models, individual and organizational effectiveness

Whether individual behaviour and organizational needs and goals can be successfully integrated depends on a variety of factors. One of the most important of these, according to many organizational psychologists (eg Schein, 1980) is the adequacy of the views that those responsible for managing the organization hold about human behaviour.

Action taken from the basis of a valid model of human behaviour is much more likely to achieve success than action based on a poor model. Thus the key to effective work performance is in the understanding of human motivation.

As Schein (1980) points out early approaches to management within organizations were based on incomplete, inadequate or just plain wrong concepts of human motivation.

The next chapter in this book explores and explains the available psychological models of human motivation.

18

2 Motivation theories and work behaviour

People differ in a variety of ways and a great deal of theory and research has been expended in efforts to understand the nature of individual differences and the underlying psychological mechanisms. Human psychological characteristics may be grouped into three major categories.

First, there are *ability* factors such as intelligence, and various aspects of skill and knowledge. Secondly, *temperamental* factors such as disposition (eg extravert, introvert) play an important role in determining behaviour. Thirdly and, in the context of this book, most important, are *motivational* factors. Motivation is concerned with the strength and direction of behaviour. As far as behaviour at work is concerned all three aspects are clearly important. Consideration of questions such as: why do people go to work, why do people work hard? clearly show that effort and performance at work are determined by ability, temperament and motivation. Despite the often complex interactions between these factors it is possible to develop theories and practical guidelines that focus specifically on motivation without losing sight of the influence of other factors.

Content and process theories

An obvious means of attempting to explain the strength and direction of behaviour (ie motivation) is to postulate that people experience certain psychological 'needs' and that when the needs are not met 'drives' to satisfy the needs are experienced.

Content theories

Some motivation theories focus explicitly on the content of motivation and attempt to develop an understanding of fundamental human needs such as physiological needs (food, water), safety and security needs and self-esteem needs. Other theories (process theories) attempt to develop understanding of the psychological process involved in motivation.

Maslow's need-hierarchy theory

One of the most influential content theories is the need hierarchy model developed by the American psychologist Abraham Maslow (Maslow, 1970). Maslow's theory of motivation claims that human motives develop sequentially according to a hierarchy of given levels of need.

1 *Physiological needs*: tissue needs such as hunger, thirst or sex.
2 *Safety needs*: needs for protection against danger, threat, deprivation.
3 *Social needs*: needs for belonging, for association, for acceptance by one's fellows, for giving and receiving friendship and love.
4 *Esteem needs*: (a) self-esteem: needs for self-confidence, for independence, for achievement; (b) esteem from others: needs for status, for recognition, for appreciation, for the deserved respect of one's fellows.
5 *Self-actualization needs*: needs for realizing one's potentialities, for continued self-development.

The hierarchical notion of the model has two related aspects. First, it assumes that the needs are activated in a sequential manner with a need at a higher level emerging only when the next lower-level need has been satisfied. Thus, safety needs emerge only after physiological needs have been satisfied, social needs after the safety needs have been satisfied, and so on right up to the self-actualization needs. Second, when a need is satisfied, it decreases in strength and ceases to dominate behaviour; the next higher need in the hierarchy then increases in strength and assumes control of behaviour. When, for example, physiological needs are satisfied, they decrease in strength and the strength of the safety needs increases.

20

The decrease in strength of a satisfied need led Maslow to assert that 'a satisfied need is not a motivation'. But this dictum applies only to the lower needs (physiological, safety, social). Satisfaction of the higher needs (esteem, self-actualization) leads to an immediate desire for more 'higher' experiences.

Maslow's theory is both a theory of developmental change and a theory of two different motivational factors. The developmental aspect of the theory states that higher needs develop when lower needs have been satisfied. The two-factor aspect of the theory is reflected in the hypothesis that lower needs decline in strength on satisfaction while higher needs grow in strength on satisfaction.

Since Maslow appeared to be more concerned with the conceptual status of his theory and less concerned with its empirical referents, he did not define his needs with precision or practicality in mind. One obstacle to an empirical testing of his theory, therefore, is the difficulty of defining the various needs in operational terms. This means that not only can there be no guarantee of an exact equivalence between the original conception of such needs as esteem and self-actualization and attempts by later researchers to define them operationally, but there is also considerable variation among the definitions used in the empirical research field. A major problem also arises in trying to infer from Maslow's writings the length of time elapsing between lower need satisfaction and higher need emergence. This could be a long period, perhaps even several years, or it could be immediate, as when a person turns directly from a satisfied lower need to an unsatisfied higher need.

A proper test of Maslow's theory would involve placing individuals who are patently in need of satisfaction on all five need levels in a situation amply supplied with the means for attaining the various satisfactions and then permitting the individuals to choose at will. Such a pure test is impossible both for ethical and practical reasons. In addition, its simplicity would not reflect the important fact that behaviour in the real world is shaped by pressures and rewards which are often beyond the individual's control; choices are invariably compromises between desires and what is feasible. Unfortunately, Maslow barely touches on the role of environmental factors in the development of his hierarchy, despite wide recognition among psychologists that behaviour can only be fully understood as a result of the interaction of individual and environmental characteristics (*see* for example Terborg, 1981). Maslow's theory holds some obvious implications for work behaviour but there are also difficulties in trying to relate the theory to work processes. One problem in trying to relate the theory to the work process lies in the fact that people do not necessarily satisfy their higher-order needs through their jobs or occupation; to test this part of the theory in formal organizations would first of all require information about all the life areas in which people seek to satisfy their higher needs. It is also worth pointing out that Maslow viewed satisfaction as the major motivational outcome of behaviour and his theory, therefore, is not manifestly relevant to productivity outcomes. What evidence is there for or against the need hierarchy theory?

One direct attempt to check Maslow's theory in an organizational setting is Hall and Nougaim's (1968) longitudinal study of 49 young managers in the American Telephone and Telegraph Company. Four of Maslow's five need categories were used in this study (physiological needs being excluded). These were:

1 *Safety needs*: defined in terms of needs for support and approval, security and structure.

2 *Affiliation needs*: similar to Maslow's social needs and defined in terms of the need to establish and maintain 'a positive affective relationship with another person or group in the work situation'.

3 *Achievement and esteem needs*: similar to Maslow's esteem needs and defined in terms of needs for achievement and challenge, and for responsibility.

4 *Self-actualization*: needs for meaning and sense of purpose, personal development, and stimulation.

Data on each manager's position on each of the need categories were derived annually for a five-year period by means of interviews. The interview protocols were then content-analysed to provide need–strength ratings ranging from 1 (low strength of need) to 3 (high strength of need) for the nine needs making up the four basic need categories. A second score was also derived to indicate the degree to which each manager was satisfied or dissatisfied in each need category. Specifically, Hall and Nougaim attempted to test Maslow's hypothesis that increases in lower need satisfaction should be related to increases in the strength of contiguous high-level needs; in other words, they attempted to check the aspect of Maslow's theory which predicts that as lower level needs are satisfied higher level needs emerge. To check this, Hall and Nougaim used three methods:

1 Static analysis involved correlating all the need satisfaction scores with all the need strength scores at the next higher level within each of the five years. High correlations were expected between safety need satisfaction and affiliation need strength, between affiliation need satisfaction and achievement-esteem need strength, and between achievement-esteem need satisfaction and self-actualization need strength.

2 Change analysis involved correlating changes in need satisfaction from one year to the next with changes in need strength at the next higher level during the same period of time. High correlations were again expected between change in satisfaction of a given need level and change in strength of the next higher need level.

3 Long-term change analysis involved comparing changes in (a) need satisfaction and (b) need strength from the first to the fifth (final) year of the investigation period for all four need levels.

The static and change analyses may be considered as tests of a relatively short time lapse between lower need satisfaction and higher need emergence, with the long-term analysis testing the longer-term emergence of the higher needs.

Neither the static nor change analyses revealed any support for Maslow's developmental hypothesis. Some support for the hypothesis was provided by the long-term change analysis in that safety need strength scores decreased significantly between the first and fifth years, while strength scores for the remainder of the needs increased significantly between the first and fifth years. (However, the increase in affiliation need strength, this being a lower need, does not accord with Maslow's theory.) No consistent pattern of change emerged from the need satisfaction scores between the first and fifth years. Overall, the results of Hall and Nougaim's study provide, at best, only modest support for Maslow's developmental theory.

Other studies designed to test Maslow's theory are reviewed in Wahba and Bridwell (1979). One test of the theory is to examine the validity of Maslow's proposal that there are *five* needs. Studies of this proposal (Wahba and Bridwell, 1979) have provided little consistent support for the theory. The general design of investigations of this issue is to generate a questionnaire which embodies items relating to all five needs. A statistical (factor) analysis of people's responses to such a questionnaire should reveal five underlying factors (needs). In practice no studies to test this proposal show all five of Maslow's proposed needs. If anything the main trend is towards three needs; lower level needs, higher level needs and self-actualization as a separate need.

As well as the proposal that there are five human needs, the other main notion in Maslow's theory is that these needs are organized into a hierarchy. Two central concepts are important here. First the *deprivation/domination* hypothesis; ie the most deficient needs should be dominant; and the *gratification-activation* proposition, ie the higher the satisfaction of a given need the lower its importance and the higher the importance of the next level need. Again, for both of these hypotheses there is no consistent support. Wahba and Bridwell comment that:

> . . . Maslow's Need Hierarchy Theory has received little clear or consistent support from the available research findings. Some of Maslow's propositions are totally rejected, while others receive mixed and questionable support at best. The descriptive validity of Maslow's Need Classification scheme is not established, although there are some indications that low-order and high-order needs may form some kind of hierarchy. However, this two-level hierarchy is not always operative, nor is it based upon the domination or gratification concepts. (p 52).

They also go on to make the point that the findings available do not necessarily invalidate Maslow's theory, but this reservation is largely because 'Maslow's Need Hierarchy Theory is almost a non-testable theory', rather than because there is any strong reason to accept the theory. In summary the available research provides little support for the theory. The evidence does provide some support for the idea that needs may be separated into higher and lower level needs and that lower needs decrease in strength as they become satisfied. Alderfer (1972) has developed a theory which incorporates three levels of need; existence, relatedness and growth (ERG) and places less emphasis on their hierarchical organization. The differences underlying lower and higher need satisfaction are further elaborated in Herzberg's (1968) two-factor theory of motivation.

Although Herzberg's theory provides some ideas about the nature of human motivation it is primarily an attempt to clarify the links between motivation and job characteristics. In view of this emphasis the theory is dealt with in more detail in chapter 3.

Process theories

Maslow's theory and to some extent Herzberg's are concerned with the *contents* (ie specific needs) of human motivational systems. An alternative, and complementary, approach to understanding motivation lies in examining the psychological *processes* that are involved in motivation. People will direct their efforts towards the goals which they value. However, the existence of a valued goal is not a sufficient condition for action; people will act only when they have a reasonable expectation that their actions will lead to desired goals.

The important role played by expectations in human behaviour has long been recognized in academic psychology but its application to the understanding of work behaviour is relatively recent. Expectancy theory states that motivation (M) is a function of the expectancy (E) of attaining a certain outcome in performing a certain act multiplied by the value (V) of the outcome for the performer:

$$M = E \times V$$

The theory predicts that outcomes which have high expectations of being realized and which are highly valued will direct the person to invest a lot of effort in his or her task. On the other hand, outcomes with high expectations and neutral or even negative values (ie disliked) will reduce the amount of effort the person is prepared to invest. Also, of course, outcomes with relatively low expectancies and/or neutral valuations will have no influence on the person's level of motivation.

Suppose that a worker desires promotion. Whether or not this leads him or her to perform at a high level will depend on the nature of his or her subjective expectations regarding the level of effort required for the desired outcome (promotion). The desire for promotion will also only lead to good performance if he or she feels there is a good probability that the organization will in fact reward performance with a promotion. On the other hand, he or she may feel that good performance will not lead to promotion. This may be because the organization promotes on the basis of seniority or formal qualifications or simply because there are no vacancies at higher levels.

The influence of subjective expectations on job performance is highlighted in a study by Lawler and Porter (1967) of managers in industrial and government organizations. They compared the performance of a group of managers who felt that pay was a probable outcome of performance with another group who felt that there was little relation between performance and pay. Rated performance was significantly higher for the former group.

Flaws with many of the earlier theories of human motivation are created by assumptions concerning the lack of individual differences between people. Content theories, such as Maslow's need hierarchy, propose that everyone's needs are organized in the same hierarchical order and to a large extent that people all strive for the same fundamental goals – such as self-actualization. Our everyday experience suggests that people may be more varied and complex than this.

A theory that proposes strong similarities between people can lead to the conclusion that there is 'one best way' to manage and motivate others. Again, any practising manager will recognize that this is simply not true. Expectancy theory is based on a more realistic, though inevitably more complex set of ideas.

First, expectancy theory recognizes that people have different types of needs, desires and goals: 'one man's meat is another's poison'.

Secondly, expectancy theory proposes that people are decision-making organisms and continually (though not necessarily consciously) make decisions about life and work-related factors, eg the amount of effort to put in to a task at work or whether promotion is worth striving for. Furthermore the theory proposes that decisions are based on people's individual perceptions of the degree to which a given behaviour will produce any specific outcome. Thus employees may value promotion (an outcome) but believe (the perception) that however hard they work it will not be recognized with promotion.

In more formal terms the main components of contemporary expectancy-valence theory utilize the concepts of *expectancy*, *instrumentality* and *valence*.

Essentially the theory suggests that the amount of effort people are prepared to put into a task depends on:

1 *Expectancy*: whether the effort will produce better performance. What is involved here is recognition of the fact that effort and performance are not always directly related. Many people could practise for 25 hours a day but never achieve the performance of Segovia or Muhammed Ali! On the other hand most people can attain a basic level of competence in quite a wide range of tasks – given that they invest some effort. Of overriding importance here is not the actual relationship between effort and performance, but what the person involved *believes* the relationship to be. Many sports coaches for example stress that an athlete's belief in his or her ability to reach certain performance targets is an essential ingredient for achievement.

2 *Instrumentality*: whether the performance, when achieved, will pay off in terms of outcomes. Thus a salesperson may decide to attempt to make contact with 25 potential new clients within the next six months. He or she may believe that, given enough effort, it may be possible to contact 25 potential clients (expectancy) but for the effort to seem worthwhile the salesperson must also believe that a portion of the new contacts will produce the desired outcome of more sales (instrumentality).

In practice it is useful to distinguish between two levels of outcome. First level outcomes are outcomes that are achieved as a direct result of performance. For example, running a 400 metres race in less than 40 seconds would win an Olympic championship. Winning an Olympic championship may, in turn, pave the way to lucrative endorsement contracts with sports-goods manufacturers (the second level outcome).

3 *Valence*: the extent to which the possible outcomes are attractive for the person concerned. This is where expectancy-valence theory provides the most explicit recognition that there are significant differences between people in terms of the outcome that they find attractive. A person who does not relish the idea of winning an Olympic gold medal will be unlikely to put in the amount of training that would lead to this outcome.

Expectancy–valence theory provides the basis of much current research and theory on motivation and work behaviour. Several studies have been conducted to investigate the validity of the ideas contained within the theory (*see* Steers and Porter, 1979, Erez, 1979).

Taken overall the studies suggest that the main components of expectancy-valence theory do influence motivation. In other words, motivation and performance are influenced by the job holder's view of the links between effort and performance (E), the perceived link between performance and outcomes (I) and the valence (V) that the outcome(s) has for the person concerned. In reality, of course, a given act of behaviour will lead to several different outcomes at the same time. For example, working hard at a job may lead to a feeling of accomplishment, high wages, recognition from management and so on. Thus the instrumentality (I) and valence (V) terms need to be summed across the total number of possible outcomes to yield an overall estimate of motivation. The theory proposes that the factors are combined in a specific (multiplicative) fashion, as in the formula:

$$\text{Motivation} = E \sum_{i=1}^{n} IV$$

An important implication of this formula is that if any term, E, I, or V, is at or near zero, for example a person places no value on the outcome (V = 0), then motivation will be at or near zero. The available research does not yet provide a firm basis for stating clearly whether this particular formula is correct or whether the factors should be combined in some other way.

Expectancy–valence theory provides some clear implications for improving motivation and performance. These implications have been presented clearly by Nadler and Lawler (1979) who divide the implications into two categories: implications for individual managers and implications for organizations. Some of the major implications are outlined below.

Implications for managers

1 Find out what particular outcomes or rewards are valued (have high valence) for each employee. The theory proposes that different people will value different rewards.

2 Be specific about the precise behaviours that constitute good levels of performance.

3 Ensure that the desired levels of performance are reachable. According to the theory, effort → performance (E → P), expectancy influences motivation. If an employee feels that it is not possible to reach the performance level, even with high effort, motivation will be low.

4 Ensure that there is a direct, clear and explicit link between performance at the desired level and outcomes/rewards. In other words, employees must be able to observe and experience the performance → outcome connection (P → O). If this is not clear and seen to work, the motivating expectancies will not be created in employees' minds.

5 Check that there are no conflicting expectancies. Once the motivating expectancies have been set up and employees have a clear grasp of the E → P and P → O relationship, it is important to check that other people or systems within the organization are not encouraging alternative expectancies. For example, another manager might be providing rewards for lower or higher levels of performance.

6 Ensure changes in outcome are large enough. As Nadler and Lawler put it, 'Trivial rewards will result in trivial amounts of effort and thus trivial improvements in performance' (p 223).

7 Check that the system is treating everyone fairly. The theory is based on the idea that people are different and therefore different rewards will need to be used for different people. Nevertheless, 'Good performers should see that

they get more of the desired rewards than do poor performers, and others in the system should see that also' (*ibid*). In other words, despite the use of different rewards the system should seem to be fair and equitable to those involved.

Implications for organizations

1 Design pay and reward systems so that:

(i) desirable performance is rewarded, eg do not reward mere 'membership' by linking pay with years of service

(ii) the relationship between performance and reward is clear. Whatever the rewards in terms of pay, promotion etc, that result from good performance, these should be made clear and explicit rather than kept ambiguous or secret.

2 Design tasks, jobs and roles so that people have an opportunity to satisfy their own needs through their work, but do not assume that everyone wants the same things. Some people may want 'enriched' jobs with greater autonomy, feedback etc, but some may not.

3 'Individualize' the organization. Expectancy theory proposes that people have different needs, valences, etc. Because of these individual differences it is important to allow people some opportunity to influence not only the type of work they do but many other aspects of organizational life, such as reward-systems, or fringe benefits offered.

Behavioural approaches

Expectancy-valence theory is a popular and influential approach to understanding and influencing motivation at work. It is not however the only approach.

Psychologists and organization behaviour specialists have developed approaches to motivation that can be divided into two broad categories. On the one hand there are theories, currently exemplified by expectancy–valence theory, which emphasize the role that internal, psychological factors, such as expectancies and values, play in determining performance at work. An alternative approach emphasizes the role of external factors, such as rewards and the influence of other people. This approach, the behavioural approach, sidesteps the issue of internal psychological factors, such as motivation, and deals directly with the factors that influence behaviour (performance) at work. The basic philosophy of the approach is summed up by Davis and Luthans (1980):

> There is today a jungle of theories that attempt to explain human behaviour in organizations. Unfortunately, many of the theoretical explanations have seemed to stray from behaviour as the unit of analysis in organizational behaviour. There is a widespread tendency for both scholars and practitioners to treat such hypothetical constructs as motivation, satisfaction and leadership as ends in themselves. We think it is time to re-emphasize the point that behaviours are the empirical reality, not the labels attached to the attempted explanation of the behaviours. (p 281).

The view that Davis and Luthans are proposing is derived from a long tradition of behaviourist research within psychology.

Instead of focusing on *motivation* as a causal construct in determining effort and performance at work, the behavioural approach argues that motivation is merely a means to an end. The end is to modify and influence behaviour at work. This philosophy is exemplified in the work of Luthans and Kreitner (1975), Davis and Luthans (1980) and O'Brien, Dickinson and Rosow (1982) on *organizational behaviour modification*. Organizational behaviour modification provides a set of procedures for directly influencing behaviour at work derived from the operant conditioning work of Skinner (1974) and more recently incorporating ideas from social learning theory (Bandura, 1977), *see also* Davis and Luthans (1980).

Conditioning and behaviour

The behavioural approach to performance improvement is based on three fundamental principles.

The first of these principles is that the focus of attention, as Davis and Luthans stress in the quotation above, should be on *observable behaviour* rather than on internal, unobservable psychological constructs such as motivation.

The second fundamental principle is that human behaviour is *learnt*. This does not mean learnt only in the narrow sense of classroom teaching but means that all of our behaviour and behaviour patterns emerge as we grow and mature from early childhood onwards. There are few if any, innate human patterns of behaviour (instincts).

The third major principle relates to the process by which this learning takes place. Behaviourists argue that specific behaviours are strengthened or weakened as a result of the *consequences* that follow behaviour. Thus, behaviour followed by rewarding consequences is more likely to be strengthened than behaviour that is followed by punishment, or produces no reward. This process of behaviour being influenced by consequences is known as operant conditioning.

Four main types of consequence can follow any behaviour and each consequence in turn has an influence on the behaviour that preceded it (see figure 5). The four major consequences are defined carefully and have quite specific meanings.

Figure 5
Consequences of behaviour and their effects

Consequence	Effect on preceding behaviour
POSITIVE REINFORCEMENT (Giving 'something nice')	Increase
NEGATIVE REINFORCEMENT (Removing 'something nasty')	Increase
PUNISHMENT (Giving 'something nasty')	Decrease
EXTINCTION (No reinforcement or punishment)	Decrease

Positive reinforcement
Reinforcement is a consequence that will increase the frequency of the behaviour that preceded it. Reinforcement can be positive or negative. Positive reinforcement is something that is rewarding for the person concerned. An important point to remember here is that there are wide

individual differences between people in the types of positive reinforcers that are rewarding. To borrow a term from expectancy–valence theory, the valences of specific consequences will vary from person to person. Thus one person will find a job with more responsibility and longer hours an acceptable reward (ie a positive reinforcement) for good performance; another person may find this unpleasant (ie a punishment). To take a more extreme example the masochist's positive reinforcement is a normal person's punishment!

Negative reinforcement

Negative reinforcement and punishment should not be confused. Like positive reinforcement, negative reinforcement will *increase* the frequency of the behaviour which preceded it. Negative reinforcement involves the removal of an unpleasant stimulus. An example of negative reinforcement described to one of the authors on a management training course may help to illustrate its meaning. The example came from a large UK organization where a recent circular from senior management had informed all members of staff that there were to be some major organizational changes in the near future. This created considerable apprehension and uncertainty amongst the employees and, as a result of this, work performance suffered and absenteeism increased. When, after several months the details of the changes were announced, although they were not to everyone's liking, work performance and absenteeism quickly returned to normal. In other words the removal of the uncertainty (an unpleasant stimulus) resulted in an increase in effective work behaviour. Thus positive and negative reinforcement serve to increase the frequency of preceding behaviour.

Punishment and extinction

Punishment and extinction decrease the frequency of behaviour. Extinction occurs when behaviour produces no reinforcing or punishing consequences. For example, the behaviour of saying good morning to someone will not continue if they consistently fail to respond.

The organizational behaviour modification system

Organizational behaviour (OB) modification involves using the principles of operant conditioning to influence the behaviour of people at work. Luthans and Kreitner (1975) have presented a procedure for this which, in outline, involves five steps:

1 Identify the critical behaviour(s) that needs to be changed
2 Measure the frequency of the critical behaviour(s)
3 Carry out a functional analysis of the behaviour(s)
4 Develop and implement an intervention strategy
5 Evaluate the effects of the intervention

Identify the critical behaviour

The first step of identifying critical behaviour(s) involves pinpointing what people actually do, or fail to do, that is worth changing. Behaviour specialists argue that it is important, at this stage, to focus on observable behaviour only. To say that someone has an unsatisfactory attitude or that their motivation is poor is not a statement of behaviour. Specific examples of behaviour such as 'arrives at work late', 'produces an unacceptable level of errors' or 'frequently misses appointments with clients' must be identified. It is also essential that the behaviour identified at this stage is important as far as individual and/or organizational performance is concerned.

Measure the frequency

Measuring the frequency of the behaviour provides a check that there really is a problem and provides some hard evidence of the position before any intervention is made, so that an accurate evaluation of change can be arrived at.

Carry out a functional analysis

The functional analysis involves identifying:

(i) the cues or stimuli that precede the behaviour, for example an employee who is consistently late when the manager is away from the office. In this case the manager's absence consistently precedes late arrival and may well be linked with lateness

34

(ii) the contingent consequences, ie the consequences in terms of reward, punishment etc that influence the behaviour concerned.

The functional analysis represents an attempt to understand the behaviour involved and perhaps provide a starting point for ideas on how to improve matters.

Develop and implement a strategy
The next stage in the process involves developing a strategy that could be used to influence work performance. Various strategies may be used but most involve the use of positive reinforcement and/or extinction to encourage good performance. Punishment for various reasons is much less useful (*see* Luthans and Kreitner, 1975; Arvey and Ivancevich, 1980).

Evaluate the effects
Evaluation can be conducted in a variety of scientific, rigorous ways (see Kazdin 1980) but for busy practising managers will most likely involve a simple examination of whether things are improved or not. Organizational behaviour (OB) modification has a good track record of successful applications although there are some technical criticisms of why OB modification works. Behaviour modification approaches do have drawbacks and limitations and some have questioned the ethics of such deliberate and controlled modification of people's behaviour (*see* Locke, 1977, Gray, 1979). There is, however, little argument that following the procedure outlined above can produce real improvements in work performance.

An illustrative study is that of Brand *et al* (1982) conducted in an agency of the United States Federal Government, the Department of Housing and Urban Development (HUD). The project as a whole shows how performance improvements are brought about through the use of OB modification in various divisions of the organization. The basic strategy employed after identifying critical behaviours was to set clear performance targets and provide praise, and interpersonal reward for a desirable performance, and feedback. Like many OB modification programmes no financial reward was used.

The programme brought about an 800 per cent increase in productivity and an increase in accuracy (from 82 per cent to

99 per cent). An important part of the programme was the provision of feedback to employees about their levels of performance.

Feedback was not limited to errors. A single chart depicted the percent of the unit's workload contributed by each employee as well as each worker's accuracy figures for the week. Review of these data uncovered some outstanding performers who had previously gone unnoticed. Employee J was found to be contributing almost 20% of the work in a 12-employee department while maintaining practically error free (99.8%) performance. The data showed that this was a truly exceptional employee, yet this man had been with the agency for 17 years without being promoted. He reported that the first time anyone had ever noticed his good work was during the current project. It would appear that he was in a high state of deprivation in terms of positive social reinforcement from his superiors. It is little wonder that a programme of feedback and praise could produce such overwhelming increases in performance in this group. (p 315).

The feedback in this case was made public; in other circumstances it may be much better to provide individual and confidential feedback. The study is one of the many examples showing the performance improvements that have been produced using OB modification techniques (see Luthans and Kreitner (1975), Hamner and Hamner (1976) and O'Brien Dickinson and Rosow (1982)). Recently OB modification specialists have begun to incorporate new theoretical ideas into their approaches. The most influential current theory is Bandura's (1977) social learning theory. Traditional behaviourist theory pays no attention to the internal, psychological processes that are involved in human performance. By contrast, social learning theory, whilst accepting the role that external events such as consequences (reinforcement etc) play in influencing behaviour, also pays specific attention to internal, psychological processes. One of the key ideas within social learning theory is that of expectancies. As Bandura has pointed out a person does not have to see his or her own house burn down to take out fire insurance. In other words we do not need to have direct experience of various consequences. We can observe what happens to others and then in turn

36

develop expectations about what may happen and how we may or may not achieve various goals.

Social learning theory recognizes that behaviour is not merely a function of the situation (ie consequences) but is also influenced by internal personal factors (expectancies, goals etc.) Social learning theorists use the term 'reciprocal determinism' to refer to the fact that personal and situational factors interact with each other and are co-determined. That is to say that people influence situations and, in turn, situations influence people.

As Robertson and Cooper (1983) point out the integration of social learning theory into the behaviourist approach may in fact provide a basis for combining expectancy–valence and behavioural approaches:

One fairly clear trend which emerges from the literature on motivation is that there is a movement away from general theories, which apply equally to everyone, towards much more individual theories of motivation, which allow for the role of individual differences. Some motivation theories emphasise internal person variables such as needs or expectancies, while others concentrate on external situation factors such as job characteristics or rewards. One of the most influential current theories of motivation emphasises the role of both person and situation variables. Expectancy theory, according to Nadler and Lawler (1979), assumes that, 'Behaviour is determined by a combination of forces in the individual and forces in the environment. Neither the individual nor the environment alone determines behaviour' (p 217). Social learning theory adopts a similar position. In fact there are many striking similarities between social learning theory and expectancy theory in their joint emphasis on expectancies, individual goals and values and the influence of both person and situation factors. In fact, if we remember that social learning theory also embodies many of the ideas of operant theory, these similarities . . . provide the basis for a synthesis between two previously irreconcilable positions concerning motivation: the behavioural, reinforcement based, operant view and the views of expectancy theory which are more concerned with internal psychological processes and their consequences. Both approaches have independently been successful in

37

improving motivation and work performance, and this emerging consensus promises even more soundly based and applicable ideas. (pp 86–87)

Goal-setting

Any approach to improving motivation and performance at work must pay attention to targets and goals that are set for employees. Numerous studies conducted in various countries have investigated the influence of goal-setting on performance, first proposed by Locke (1968). This body of evidence has shown that, provided a goal relates to the performance criteria being used (eg a safety goal matches safety performance factors), and the goal is accepted by an individual, virtually any type of action that is able to be measured and controlled can be improved. Locke's fundamental idea is that realistic, hard, specific goals produce better performance than easy goals or no goals. Goals have been demonstrated to affect performance through four mechanisms: (a) directing attention and action, (b) mobilizing effort, (c) increasing task persistence, and (d) motivating the search for appropriate performance strategies.

Two relevant goal attributes, content and intensity, are of particular importance. Goal content refers to features such as the level of goal difficulty and how specific the goal is, while goal intensity refers to the perceived importance of and strength of commitment to a goal.

Goal difficulty is related to arousal and effort. When difficult goals are accepted by employees, they will mobilize and expend more effort toward reaching the goal than when goals are easy. This is because individuals use more of their total capacity (eg skills and experience) under high demand, as opposed to low demand, conditions. Difficult goals are typically determined by performance levels achieved by relatively few individuals, compared with performance levels usually obtained by the majority of employees, within a particular work situation (eg production norms).

The specificity of a goal is related to the mechanisms for directing attention and action. The directional effects of goals are twofold: the first, known as 'orientation', causes the individual to focus upon the particular activities and resources needed to achieve a goal. The second effect, 'activation', causes the individual to activate relevant knowledge and skills (Locke *et al*, 1989). Provided employees are committed to a goal, and are actively trying to achieve it, the goal mechanisms of effort, persistence and direction, function on a relatively automatic basis (Locke and Latham, 1990). However, if employees believe that these attributes on their own are not enough to achieve a goal, they may adopt a different task performance strategy. Task strategies are deliberate action plans motivated by goals that have independent effects upon performance, depending on the complexity of the task. For complex tasks increased effort will not be translated into productivity gains unless effective strategies are developed for deploying that effort productively. For example, a machine operator who is inadequately trained may not be able to reach his or her production targets even with intense effort; training would provide the task strategies to enable the effort to be translated into performance. Information about different strategies may come from past experience with the task, direct instruction, strategy training, priming or role modelling.

Although the processes of choosing and committing oneself to a goal are related, and many factors that influence goal choice also influence goal commitment, they are two distinct facets. Goal choice is a function of (a) what the individual expects can be achieved, (b) what the individual would ideally like to achieve and (c) what the individual believes is the minimum that should be achieved. Locke and Bryan (1968) demonstrated that the minimum goal typically regulates performance most closely, rather than the expected or ideal goal.

Factors influencing an employee's choice of goal, owing to their perceived performance capability, include their levels of past performance, their ability or skill, whether or not they have succeeded or failed in reaching previous goals, self-efficacy (*see* also page 41), and their expectations of achieving the goal. Factors influencing goal choice through the perceived desirability of reaching a goal include group norms (eg production norms), group goals, peer pressure and encouragement, role modelling, competition, value of achievement, incentives, feedback, and dissatisfaction.

Difficult goals lead to higher performance only when an individual is committed to them (Locke and Latham, 1990). Thus goal commitment is significantly related to performance

(Erez and Zidon, 1984) in that, as commitment declines, performance also declines. Many factors influence and affect goal commitment, including goal difficulty level, the assignment of goals by an authority figure, participatively setting goals, peer group influence, stating the goals publicly, the provision of incentives and rewards, feedback, and goal conflict.

Commitment to a goal can be considerably improved if employees participate in the goal-setting process. Research suggests that, for many people, a goal set and delegated by others serves as a disincentive, which may lead to the rejection of goals (Naylor *et al*, 1980). However, Latham *et al* (1988) suggest that participation in goal-setting is not crucial so long as a determined effort is made to 'sell' the goals after they have been decided upon.

In a study that compared assigned and participative goal-setting in relation to the improvement of safety on construction sites in the UK, Cooper *et al* (1992) found that on sites where operatives participated in the goal-setting process there was better performance, compared with sites where goals were assigned. In many organizations goal-setting is part and parcel of the performance appraisal process, and research suggests that in appraisal interviews there is a positive link between inviting the subordinate to participate in goal-setting and the subordinate's satisfaction with the appraisal review (Nemeroff and Wexley, 1979) which may be related to perceptions of procedural fairness (Tyler and Bies, 1990).

Acceptance of and commitment to goals is a crucial factor in performance, as demonstrated by Erez and Zidon (1984), who found that, when goals are accepted, difficult goals lead to better performance than easy goals. When goals are rejected, however, the relationship between goal difficulty and performance is reversed. Encouraging participation and acceptance of goals does not mean that employees should be given complete freedom to set their own goals, but that targets should be arrived at by a process of sensible and realistic discussion. Taking part in discussions to decide the target level to be achieved not only makes it clear to employees how difficult and specific the goal should be but also clarifies for all parties concerned the best strategy to adopt, and what resources may be needed to maximize goal achievement. For example, there is not much point in setting employees a target to produce 20 per cent extra widgets if the extra materials necessary to produce the widgets are not available. Further benefits derived from participation include 'ownership' of the improvement process on the part of employees, improved working relations between employees and employers, improved job satisfaction, and the reduction of perceived conflicts between competing organizational goals (eg safety *v.* productivity), which over a period of time may lead to the setting of higher goals (Austin and Bobko, 1985).

The provision of performance feedback, usually defined as 'information about the effectiveness of one's work behaviour' (Taylor *et al*, 1984), is a necessary condition for goals to have their full effects (Erez, 1977). The relationship between goals and feedback is complex, in that goals mediate the effectiveness of feedback, and feedback moderates the effectiveness of goals. In combination they are complementary and far more effective than either of them alone. This relationship can be construed as the joint effects of motivation and cognition, which control action (Locke and Latham, 1990). In other words, goals inform individuals to achieve particular levels of performance, in order for them to direct and evaluate their actions, while performance feedback allows the individual to track how well he or she is doing in relation to the goal, so that, if necessary, adjustments in effort, direction or possibly task strategies can be made. Thus feedback involves information and informs individuals as to what their current status is, while goals involve evaluation and tell individuals what is desirable.

Goals, expectancies and self-efficacy

At first sight an examination of the research on goal-setting and expectancy suggests an apparent contradiction. The contradiction appears to arise when the relationships between goal difficulty, expectancy of success and performance are examined. The relations between goal difficulty and performance are shown in figure 6. Research has shown that as goal difficulty increases so does performance (Locke *et al*, 1981).

Expectancy, usually operationalized as 'subjective probability of success', also shows a clear relationship with performance (see figure 6a). As the subjective probability of success increases, so does performance. The relationship between goal difficulty and subjective probability of success is, however,

41

Figure 6
The relationship between goal difficulty and performance

Figure 6a
The relationship between subjective probability of success and performance

Figure 6b
The relationship between goal difficulty and subjective probability of success

negative (see figure 6b and Garland, 1984). In other words, as goal difficulty increases, the subjective probability of success decreases. Taken alone, this finding (ie harder goals are seen as less likely to be achieved) is intuitively reasonable. When all three relationships shown in figure 6 are considered together there is an internal contradiction.

Locke et al (1986) resolved these apparent contradictions between expectancy theory and goal-setting theory in two ways, based upon propositions put forward by Garland (1984) and Bandura (1982). Garland (1984) noted that in studies using different levels of goal difficulty (eg high, medium and low) the links between subjective probability of success (SPS) and performance had been examined by combining data for all levels of goal difficulty, rather than by examining SPS–performance links separately at each level of goal difficulty. Thus the expectancy of 'goal attainment' meant different things to different groups. He conducted a reanalysis of some previous studies and examined the SPS-performance links separately for different levels of goal difficulty. For easy goals there was no relationship between SPS and performance. For medium and high goals, however, there was a clear relationship between SPS and performance. It was only between different levels of goal difficulty that a negative relationship was observed, which is a result of incorrect data analysis. Locke et al (1984) produced similar results. In situations where goals are easy it seems likely that SPS is high for all performers, and therefore a link between SPS is unlikely to appear. When goals are difficult, as predicted by expectancy–valence theory, there should be, and is, a relationship between SPS and performance. Garland also used a different statistical technique (multiple regression, rather than zero-order correlations) to examine the links between goal difficulty, SPS and performance. The findings of the analysis also showed that goal difficulty and SPS are both related to performance.

Self-efficacy, defined by Bandura (1982) as 'how well one can execute courses of action required to deal with prospective situations' (p 122), closely resembles the effort to performance expectancies in expectancy–valence theory, in that both these concepts are more strongly related to future than to past performance. Self-efficacy is broader in meaning than expectancy in that it encompasses the estimate of an individual's total capacity (eg ability, skills, effort, adaptability to situational constraints, etc) to perform at a given level. The second resolution of the conflict between expectancy theory and goal theory was based upon the way in which expectancy was measured. Expectancy measures typically measured the probable chances of success given the degree of effort needed to succeed, which implicitly included a belief in the individual's total ability to perform. Self-efficacy measures explicitly explore individuals' belief in their total capacity to perform. Thus more recent expectancy measures have incorporated a wider range of criteria, which include explicit belief in one's total capacity. This has resulted in better predictions of performance than expectancies measured in other ways (Ilgen *et al*, 1981).

Locke *et al* (1984) explored the links between self-efficacy, goals and performance, and found that self-efficacy was positively related to goal level, goal commitment (when the goal was self-set) and performance, both within and between groups. They concluded that, the higher the efficacy, the higher the performance.

Another related aspect, derived from Bandura's (1982) social learning theory, which has been integrated into goal theory is that of role modelling. In essence, observing high-performing role models leads individuals to set higher performance goals, increasing commitment to those goals and enhancing self-efficacy, than does observing a low-performing role model (Weiss and Rakestraw, 1988), although these effects disappear as individuals gain experience at the task. Other research has shown that self-modelling has even stronger effects on performance than modelling by others or monetary incentives (Dowrick and Hood, 1981). This suggests that if a high-performing role model is available employees will model themselves upon the individual concerned until the behaviour has been internalized. When they feel confident in their own abilities, they become self-motivated to set themselves even more difficult goals.

Setting realistic goals

Given that goal-setting has been demonstrated to improve performance, within certain boundary conditions, how is it put into operation? The procedure is similar in many respects to that of organizational behaviour modification, except for the goal-setting procedure. Goal-setting may be undertaken with groups or individual employees. In the examples that follow, goal-setting is discussed in the context of groups, although the procedure is the same for individuals.

Identify the problem

The first step involves deciding upon what it is that is to be improved. This is typically determined by the identification of a specific organizational problem that is constantly arising, although not necessarily so. By analysing company records it is possible to identify a number of areas where the company as a whole would benefit from performance improvement. For example, what is the ratio of enquiries to products and converted sales? What is the ratio of fuel used to miles travelled for the company fleet of vans and cars? What is the ratio of materials' wastage to the end product? Is there a problem with employee safety or occupational health?

Identify the performance indicators

Once an area has been identified for improvement, it is necessary to identify the particular behaviours or situations that are crucial to performance. For example, if fuel consumption appears to be excessive, it may be due to the drivers' style (eg heavy use of the accelerator, not using the gears correctly, heavy braking) or it may be due to insufficient or inappropriate vehicle maintenance. Further, it may be a combination of the two. Either way, goals could be set to improve both. The critical behaviour identified would then form an objective basis for a performance indicator, used to measure subsequent performance.

Measure performance

Once the performance indicator has been established and written in behaviour-specific terms, in order for the criteria of performance to be assessed consistently across employees, performance is measured for a period of time, to provide a baseline by which goals can be set and future performance compared.

Goal-setting procedures

In practical terms, during the goal-setting process, generating high goal commitment and subsequent performance may best be achieved by following certain procedures, such as:

1 The results of the baseline measure should be displayed on a feedback chart of some description. An explanation as to why improvements in the particular area of job performance are necessary, how the performance indicator was obtained and developed, and how it is to be used, should be given. The goal-setter should not only emphasize that the baseline measure is the current performance level and that performance can and should be increased, but also emphasize the benefits of reaching the goals – to the employees themselves, as well as to the company.

2 Stress the importance of employees participating in the setting of a difficult, specific but realistic goal to improve performance. This encourages commitment to and acceptance of goals and also minimizes the likelihood of resistance.

3 Emphasize that sometimes goals are set unrealistically high and therefore not expected to be achieved. Goal-setting only works if the goals are perceived as realistic and attainable.

4 Stress that no penalties will be applied for not reaching the goal. This ensures positive action. Research has shown that employees are likely to test this element. If sanctions are applied, it is probable that employees will reject the goals, with subsequent detrimental effects upon performance.

5 Emphasize the necessary actions that will enable the employees to reach the goal. This helps to clarify the particular behaviours that are required.

6 Ask the employees to set a difficult, specific goal that the majority agree with. If the goal appears to be too easy, suggest a more difficult one. Essentially this is a period of negotiation between management and employees, the outcome of which should be satisfactory to both parties.

7 Explain to the employees that, as performance is monitored, the results will be posted on the feedback chart at

regular intervals, and that the chart will be placed in a prominent position in the workplace.

8 Ensure that an authority figure who is supportive, but who will exert reasonable pressure on subordinates to reach the goals set, is present during the goal-setting session. Management commitment to the intervention is of extreme importance. Many organizational interventions have floundered because managerial commitment was lacking.

Control theory

Control theory is a motivational theory of self-regulation (Campion and Lord, 1982; Carver and Scheir, 1982) that originally attempted to integrate behaviourism, cybernetics and goal-setting. Subsequently Klein (1989) expanded the model to incorporate elements of attribution theory, expectancy theory, feedback theory and information processing theory, which he postulated to form the basis of a 'meta-theory' or framework by which specific motivational issues might be addressed. It is derived directly from the 'Test Operate, Test Exit' (TOTE) model of multiple feedback loops in skill acquisition theory (Miller *et al*, 1960). The theory postulates that there is an input (i.e. feedback) which is detected by a sensor. The input is fed into a comparator (conscious judgement), which compares it to a reference standard (ie goal). If there is a 'deviation or disturbance', a signal is sent to an effector, which generates modified output (action). The modified output then becomes the input for the next cycle. Thus self-regulation is based on the notion of a negative closed feedback loop.

The model further incorporates the concept of a hierarchical goal structure (Carver and Scheier, 1981) which specifies the process by which goals gain importance. For example, an individual's overall goal of gaining corporate membership of a professional body can be broken down into sub-goals, such as studying for appropriate qualifications, and completing a minimum period of practice to obtain sufficient professional experience. The sub-goal of studying for qualifications can be broken down further to other sub-goals, such as being admitted to an institution of learning, attending lectures, completing course work, passing exams, etc. When lower-order sub-

47

goals have been attained, the next goal in the hierarchy becomes dominant, and so on until the overall goal is attained.

The model has, however, attracted criticism on the issue of discrepancy reduction. For example, the notion that the main motivator of action is the removal of discrepancies or disturbancies between goals and feedback implies that the model naturally maintains a steady state. Goal-setting, however, is essentially a feed-forward discrepancy-creating process (Nuttin, 1984; Bandura and Cervone, 1983). If the steady-state hypothesis were correct, an individual would simply adapt goals to levels indicated by the feedback, to guarantee no disturbance or discrepancy, which would mean that the model had no motivational value. The removal of discrepancies is a correlate of goal-directed action, not the cause. The causal sequence begins with setting the goal, not with removing deviations from it (Locke and Latham, 1990).

Despite this criticism, if one accepts that goals are the major motive for action, the model is an impressive attempt to explain the boundary conditions that underlie motivational processes. Many hypotheses derived from the model have been claimed to address issues that other theories have failed to explain (Klein, 1989). While empirical evidence has generally been supportive (eg Ashford, 1989; Kernon and Lord, 1990;), much research is still needed to validate this approach to motivation.

Equity

The notion of fair play, or, more explicitly, equity, is an important concept in work motivation. The basic premise is that employees seek fairness and justice in social exchange relationships, between themselves and employers. Perceived unfairness or injustice will create psychological tension. This will be revealed in the form of detrimental effects upon task and organizational goals though poor performance (Greenberg, 1990).

Two main forms of fairness have been identified. First, distributive fairness (Adams, 1965), which is concerned with the distribution and allocation of outcomes, dependent upon an individual's input. This type of equity can be applied to motivation in two main ways. First, individuals need to feel that they are getting fair treatment at work in terms of their inputs, eg skills, experience, effort, etc, and the outcomes they receive, eg pay, praise, promotion, etc. Secondly, people need to feel that they are being treated fairly when they compare themselves with others. Employees working long hours on a difficult, demanding and highly skilled task will, in most cases, feel that they should benefit more than those working shorter hours on an easier task.

The second type of equity is procedural fairness, which refers to perceptions about procedures used in organizations to make decisions concerning outcomes. It has been argued that perceptions of procedural fairness can be enhanced, independently of the outcomes obtained, by providing individuals with the opportunity to exert an influence over the decision-maker. The motivational strength of perceived procedural unfairness appears to lie in its relation to an individual's valued goals. A person striving for a highly valued goal is less likely to be affected by procedural unfairness than when a goal is not valued. Unfairness in the latter case is likely to lead to poor performance. When applied to procedures such as performance appraisal or performance evaluation, if the procedure is perceived and interpreted by the employee as a means to an end, rather than as an end in itself, perceptions of distributive fairness have more influence than procedural fairness (Greenberg, 1987). Closely linked with perceptions of procedural unfairness is the role played by interpersonal factors (Tyler and Bies, 1990). Five factors that contribute to perceptions of fairness, are suggested. These are:

1 Adequate consideration of an employee's viewpoint.

2 Suppression of personal bias towards the employee.

3 Applying criteria consistently across employees.

4 Providing early feedback to employees concerning the outcome of decisions.

5 Providing employees with an adequate explanation for the decision made.

Adherence to these factors should enhance motivational effects, through commitment and choice, in the direction and intensity of effort allocated by an employee to task and organizational goal attainment.

An integration

Several approaches to motivation and work performance have been dealt with in this chapter. Each approach has its own specific areas of emphasis and implications. At times different approaches may relect somewhat conflicting views. Although there are differences there is also a significant amount of common ground and it is possible to draw out several common practical guidelines. Chapter 7 provides some specific guidance on the practical aspects of improving motivation by implementing ideas discussed throughout this book and in particular the theoretical issues discussed in this chapter.

3 Work characteristics that motivate

Modern organizations are increasingly required to pay attention to a broad and often complex set of issues concerning job design. One of the basic problems for organizations to resolve concerns the relationships between job satisfaction, job performance and efficiency. As chapter 1 highlights, early work on job design emphasizes the search for efficiency – sometimes at the expense of job satisfaction. Lupton and Tanner (1980) have described the dilemma confronting work designers:

> The designer of a manufacturing system is likely to be confronted with the problem of reconciling conflicting aims and values, especially if he is charged with the task of providing a high quality of work life for those who will man the system. Although it is conceivable that in a given case all the aims are consistent, logic and the experience of practitioners combine to show that there is no necessary connection of cause and effect between efficiency and the quality of working life. (p 218).

Attempts to resolve this dilemma in a humane as well as an efficient manner are described in chapter 6. Here we will be concerned with the characteristics of work that are important in determining levels of motivation, satisfaction and performance.

Before looking in more detail at the relevant characteristics of jobs, it is useful to make a distinction between characteristics that are concerned with the actual activities or *tasks* involved in the job and characteristics concerned with the *context* in which the job is conducted (eg the work group, technology, organization structure and climate – *see* chapter

1). The first part of this current chapter discusses task characteristics.

Tasks

Hackman (1969) defines a task as:

> a stimulus complex and a set of instructions which specify what is to be done vis-a-vis the stimuli. The instructions indicate what operations are to be performed by the subject(s) with respect to the stimuli and/or what goal is to be achieved.

Various other definitions of tasks have been offered. Fine and Wiley (1974) for example, describe a task as an action, or action sequence, organized over time and designed to contribute to a specific result or objective. Annett et al (1971) break tasks down into operations: 'Any unit of behaviour, no matter how long or short its duration and no matter how simple or complex its structure, which can be defined in terms of its objectives'. In short, although there are differences of emphasis and detail, a task is represented by a statement of what actions are to be carried out and what end results are to be achieved.

Jobs are made up of collections of tasks and the starting point for understanding any job is to conduct a thorough analysis of the job. The development and refinement of job analysis techniques has been a major activity of occupational psychologists for many decades and a variety of techniques are available for conducting job analyses. These vary from several highly technical and sophisticated procedures through to more rudimentary but, nevertheless, useful methods. Smith and Robertson (1986) present a basic six step approach which provides a straightforward but robust method for analysing jobs.

Step one: collect together documents such as the training manual, which give information concerning the job.

Step two: ask the relevant manager about the job. Ask about the main purposes of the job, the activities involved and the personal relationships which must be maintained with others.

Step three: ask the job holder similar questions about the job. In some circumstances, it might be possible to persuade the job holder to keep a detailed record of work activities over a period of one or two weeks.

Step four: observe the job holder performing the work and make a note of the most important points.

Step five: attempt to do the job yourself. Of course, it will be impossible to follow all of these steps for every job. For example, it would be dangerous for anyone but a skilled worker to operate some types of machinery. In other jobs the main activities are mental work which cannot be directly observed.

Step six: write the job description. When the information has been collected, the results are set out in the job description. There is no single format which is better than others. However, the types of items described in figure 7 have been found to be very useful and can be used with little prior knowledge. Information about the job is grouped under six headings. In general, job descriptions should stick to specifying the results which should be achieved. Prescriptions of *how* the job is to be done should be avoided: working methods or conditions may change and individual workers may achieve their targets in different ways. Smith and Robertson (1986) suggest that the approach outlined above is well within the competence of any intelligent manager or personnel specialist.

Other approaches to job analysis are outlined in figure 8 together with a list of advantages and disadvantages. Blum and Naylor (1968) and Smith and Robertson provide more information on the approaches outlined in figure 8.

Figure 7
The job description

In general, job descriptions should cover:

1 Identification of the job
Job title
Location, eg department
Number of people in job
Who the job holder is responsible to
Who the job holder is responsible for

2 Purpose of the job
A brief and unambiguous statement of the main purposes of the job and the reason why the job exists.

53

Figure 7 – contd.

3 **Responsibilities** (or key results)
What responsibilities does the job holder have for people, material, money? Generally, this section contains a list of the end results that must be achieved. *It is important that these end results are quantified wherever possible* so that it is clear if either quantity or quality are not achieved.

With managers, these key result areas will concern:

product produced to a programme
utilization of resources in an efficient way
quality of output
personnel, especially the handling and development of subordinates.

For managers, it may also be necessary to specify:
(1) the numbers and levels of *people controlled* and the degree of control, eg part time or full time supervision, recruitment, development, discipline, dismissal, salary determination.

(ii) financial aspects such as:
budgetary or cost control
type and value of assets, including stock
responsibility for sales
purchasing or investment
responsibility for forecasting and planning.

(iii) guidance, how much supervision can be expected.

4 **Relationships**
Who does the job holder work with? What is the nature of each relationship – liaison, delegation, etc?

Figure 8
Advantages and disadvantages of nine methods of job analysis

1 **Questionnaire method**
Advantages
Good for producing quantitative information and can produce objective and generalizable results; cheap.
Disadvantages
Substantial sample needed; substantial foreknowledge needed to be able to construct questionnaire; respondents must be able and willing to give accurate replies.

2 Checklist method

Similar to questionnaire method but since responses are either YES or NO the result may be 'cruder' or require larger sample. They tend to require fewer subjective judgements.

3 Individual interviews

Advantages
Very flexible; can provide in-depth information; easy to organize and prepare.
Disadvantages
Time consuming; expensive; difficult to analyse.

4 Observation interviews

Similar to individual interview method but provides additional information, eg visual or auditory information. The higher level of contextual cues makes it more difficult for the analyst to be misled. The method may expose both the analyst and the worker to increased safety hazards.

5 Group interviews

Similar to the individual interview but they are less time consuming for analyst and some claim that richer information is obtained since interviewees stimulate each others' thoughts. They are more difficult to organize and there is the danger that a group is over-influenced by one individual.

6 Technical conference method

Advantages
Quick, cheap and can be used for jobs that do not yet exist. Can avoid restrictive practices.
Disadvantages
The 'experts' may not be true experts and an unrealistic analysis may result.

7 Diary method

Advantages
Cheap, flexible and requires little advance preparation. Useful for non-manual tasks where observation is of limited value. Can also be used in jobs involving a wide variety of tasks.
Disadvantages
Needs cooperation from respondents; tendency to keep incomplete logs and frequent but minor items often omitted.

Figure 8 – contd.

8 Work participation method
Advantages
Can produce very realistic analyses.
Disadvantages
Expensive, time consuming and can only be used for jobs requiring short training and no safety hazards.

9 Critical incident method
Advantages
Focuses on the aspects of a job that are crucial to success.
Disadvantages
Often produces incomplete data which are difficult to analyse.

Job characteristics and motivation

The links between the characteristics (eg the tasks) of jobs and motivation are important, and an understanding of these links provides a basis for designing jobs that are both satisfying and motivating. One of the more widely known attempts to link job characteristics with human motivation, satisfaction and performance is Herzberg's two-factor theory.

Herzberg has expressed his theory largely in terms of satisfaction outcomes and he has been less explicit about productivity outcomes. He states that we normally think of satisfaction and dissatisfaction as opposite ends of the same continuum but that they are really two completely different concepts. In Herzberg's view, the factors which create satisfaction (variously called satisfiers or motivators) are those which stem from the intrinsic content of the job (eg challenge, meaning) and which satisfy the higher needs, whereas the factors which create dissatisfaction (variously called dissatis- fiers or hygiene factors) are those which stem from the extrinsic job context (eg pay, supervision) and which satisfy the lower needs. Like Maslow, Herzberg asserts that higher-need satisfaction is self-sustaining. However, his treatment of lower-need satisfaction differs somewhat from the writers we have already discussed. Dissatisfaction stems from ungratified lower needs but, and here is the important point, gratified lower needs do not produce satisfaction, they merely remove dissatisfaction.

The motivator–hygiene theory originated in an interview investigation of 203 accountants and engineers who were asked to describe specific occasions when they felt exceptionally good or exceptionally bad about their jobs. Analysis of the interview responses revealed that the good occasions were characterized by intrinsic features of the job (achievement, recognition, the work itself, responsibility, advancement), while the bad occasions were characterized by extrinsic job features (company policy and administration, supervision, salary, relations with co-workers, working conditions). Specifically, in the good experiences intrinsic sources were mentioned nearly four times as often as extrinsic sources (78 per cent against 22 per cent); in the bad experiences, extrinsic sources were mentioned almost twice as often as intrinsic sources (64 per cent against 36 per cent). Many subsequent studies, using the same 'story-telling' technique, have produced similar results.

Herzberg's theory has been roughly handled by academic critics. They complain that the two-factor nature of the theory is essentially an artefact of the interview technique used by Herzberg and his supporters. People are more likely to attribute such experiences as achievement and recognition to themselves and to attribute dissatisfying experiences to external aspects of their environment. It is true that those studies which have used the story-telling technique have provided the strongest support for the theory, but studies employing quite different methods of attitude assessment have produced evidence which is at least partly consistent with the two-factor formulation. A possible reason for differences in the findings of the various attempts to check the two-factor theory is that the theory has been formulated in different ways by different investigators. It has been pointed out that there are at least five different ways of expressing the theory, each of which puts a slightly different slant on it.

It is worth noting that Herzberg does not describe the specific contents in jobs that lead to satisfaction but rather refers to processes (eg achievement, recognition) which result from behaviour; in other words, he tends to talk in terms of outcomes rather than means. A further methodological shortcoming of Herzberg's approach lies in its emphasis on satisfaction/dissatisfaction criteria to the extent of neglecting behavioural criteria such as performance, absenteeism and labour turnover. A rigorous theory of job motivation must include both behavioural and satisfaction criteria.

Two points emerge from the various studies which have examined Herzberg's two-factor theory. First, there is some support for the idea of intrinsic and extrinsic job factors contributing separately to satisfaction. Secondly, there is no consensus that the two sets of factors affect satisfaction in the qualitatively different ways hypothesized by Herzberg.

Herzberg's approach deals with both *task* and *context* factors that influence motivation and performance. There is a series of studies and theories, by various investigators, that focus much more specifically on task factors.

Task characteristics

Two sets of ideas that have had significant impact on subsequent workers are those of Turner and Lawrence (1965) and Cooper (1973).

The classic work of Turner and Lawrence identifies six important characteristics known as 'requisite task attributes':

1 variety (for example, in tools, equipment, machinery used, in prescribed work pace)
2 autonomy (for example, amount of latitude in determining the method of work)
3 required interactions (contact necessary for proper task performance)
4 optional interaction (possibilities or limitations (eg due to noise) of contact both on and off the job)
5 knowledge and skill (learning time necessary)
6 responsibility (for example, ambiguity of remedial action).

In addition, Turner and Lawrence distinguish a number of other attributes which they call 'associated task attributes' and which are closely associated with the job but not required for task performance.

Cooper (1973) makes important contributions to the development of ideas concerning task characteristics. His framework outlines four conceptually distinct job dimensions: variety, discretion, contribution and goal characteristics.

Variety

Cooper uses the term variety to describe the amount of physical differentiation in the job and its immediate surroundings: differentiation in prescribed work pace; in physical location of work; in prescribed work operations, and in the number of people available for interaction in the working area. The variety here is essentially among the prescribed and known features of the job.

There is evidence from industrial studies to support the hypothesis that holders of jobs characterized by limited variety will experience dissatisfaction (boredom) and that the need to introduce more variation from sources external to the task will lead to reduced performance and increased absenteeism and labour turnover.

Much of the early research on boredom in work carried out by the former Industrial Fatigue Research Board was concerned with the effects of limited variety in the job and ways to increase the amount of variety in order to reduce boredom. Wyatt, Fraser and Stock (1928) present evidence from a number of quasi-experimental industrial studies to support the view that more varied work leads to greater productivity and that less varied work leads to greater variability of output and less liking for the task. However, in certain tasks studied by Wyatt and his colleagues, such as soap-packing and assembling parts for recording instruments, although the more varied conditions generally resulted in greater liking, they led to decreased output. The explanation for this lay apparently in the less efficient sequencing of operations in the more varied conditions.

Walker and Guest (1952) found that highly repetitive jobs (ie those low in variety) in automobile assembly were the ones most disliked. Turner and Lawrence (1965), in a comprehensive study of 47 different jobs held by 470 workers in 11 industries, report that their several measures of variety were negatively related to absenteeism. They also report that cycle time, regarded here as an aspect of variety, was similarly non-related to absences. However, they found no significant relationships between their variety characteristics.

Cooper did not feel that variety was a true motivator. Its value was probably limited to routine, repetitive jobs which characteristically induce feelings of boredom. Therefore an increase in variety would simply mean a decrease in boredom.

Discretion

Cooper uses discretion to mean being free to exercise choice. Discretion in work takes two forms: choice in organizing the means and tools of one's work; and choice in solving problems with the appropriate knowledge. He called the former, means discretion and the latter, skill discretion.

In skilled work, the two forms of discretion are related in that the successful application of skill discretion depends upon the freedom to manipulate the back-up operations (ie means discretion) as required. Cooper's views corresponded with those expressed by Blauner (1964):

> The freedom to determine techniques of work, to choose one's tools and to vary the sequence of operations, is part of the nature and traditions of craftsmanship. Because each job is somewhat different from previous jobs, problems continually arise which require a craftsman to make decisions. Traditional skill thus involves the frequent use of judgement and initiative, aspects of a job which give the worker a feeling of control over his environment.

In semi-skilled work, because of its largely routine non-problematic nature, little skill discretion exists. Semi-skilled work does, however, offer some scope for the exercise of choice in the way that methods, tools and pace of work are used.

Of the several task attributes studied by Turner and Lawrence (1965), those which specially characterized discretion (autonomy, responsibility, knowledge and skill) were most significantly and negatively related to absenteeism. It is also noteworthy that the only task attributes related significantly and positively to job satisfaction were again those defining discretion (responsibility, knowledge and skill, and optional interaction off the job). (This finding held true only for town workers; in the case of city workers no significant relationships were found between these task attributes and job satisfaction.)

Contribution

Most work results in constructive changes which contribute to some end, whether this is a product, service or new knowledge. Cooper argues that contributions derive their motivational value from the fact that they effect changes within the total structure of the task; the greater the contribution to the total task, the greater its power to motivate. In addition, the effects of contributions must be noticed by the performer in order to maximize the impact that they have. Contributions, then, can be viewed first in terms of their effectance value or the extent to which they contribute to the total task and, secondly, in terms of their feedback or the distinctness of their perceived effects.

A common assertion embodying the idea of contribution is that 'whole' tasks, in contrast to 'part' tasks, are more motivating and more satisfying to perform. Cooper points out that it is not the fact of 'wholeness' that is important but the significance of the contribution within the overall structure of the product or service. Consider the task of completing a jigsaw puzzle. Our imaginary performer begins by selecting all those pieces having at least one straight side; his strategy is to complete first the outside frame of the puzzle and then fill in the middle 'picture' pieces. In these early stages the fitting together of each jigsaw piece does not add spectacularly to the total puzzle but, as the salient characteristics of the picture emerge, each added piece contributes more significantly to the task, its significance being proportional to the extent of the information it adds. Many organizational jobs are like this. Compare the job of press operator in a car factory whose machine presses out car doors from sheet steel with the job of the assembler who fixes the same doors to the visible car body. The latter job contributes centrally to the total configuration of the product whereas the former contributes only peripherally. Adding a door or steering column or a wheel all represent important contributions to the manufacture of the vehicle. Early production contributions have little value because they do not contribute visibly to the vehicle's essential character. Equally, contributions which come late in the production process add relatively little because at this stage the vehicle's essential character has been established for some time.

61

Turner and Lawrence (1965) used the concept of task identity, a composite of both contribution value and feedback, as a means of distinguishing a task 'as a unique and visible work assignment'. They found that, while task identity was negatively associated with absenteeism, it was unrelated to job satisfaction. Hackman and Lawler (1971) used task identity (which they defined largely in terms of the extent to which the employee can do a 'whole' piece of work) and feedback as separate task characteristic measures. In their study, task identity was significantly related to: rated overall performance effectiveness (0.11, $p < 0.05$), absenteeism (-0.22 $p < 0.05$), and various specific satisfaction items such as 'feeling of worthwhile accomplishment' (0.28, $p < 0.05$) and 'self-esteem obtained from job' (0.15, $p < 0.05$). In contrast, feedback was neither related to performance nor absenteeism but was clearly related to items such as 'feeling of worthwhile accomplishments' (0.42, $p < 0.05$) and 'self-esteem obtained from job' (0.35, $p < 0.05$).

Goal characteristics

As far as goals are concerned Cooper suggests that although the *contents* of specific goals may be motivating in themselves, two other features of goals are also important. These are the *clarity* and *difficulty* of the goal.

Subsequent research has explored these ideas and investigated in some depth the role that goals play in motivation (*see* chapter 2).

The job (task) characteristics combined

Writing on the Bell Telephone System's experience with job design, Robert Ford (1969) has suggested that job characteristics have to combine in order to motivate employees: 'Perhaps they have the effect of a shotgun blast; it is the whole charge that brings the beast down'. But exactly how do they combine?

The most widely used and influential contemporary model that attempts to explain the combined links between job characteristics and personal and work outcomes such as

motivation, satisfaction and performance is the job characteristics model of Hackman and Oldham (1975, 1976, 1980).

The job characteristics model

An examination of the job characteristics model shows clearly
that it has its origins in the earlier work of Turner and
Lawrence (1965), Cooper (1973) and Hackman and Lawler
(1971).

The core of the job characteristics model is a set of proposals
concerning the relationships between a specific set of job
characteristics, a set of intervening psychological states and
various personal and work outcomes (such as work motivation and performance). Figure 9 provides an overview of the
main components of the job characteristics model.

Figure 9
The job characteristics model
(adapted from Hackman and Oldham, 1976)

Core job dimensions	Critical psychological states	Personal and work outcomes
Skill variety Task identity Task significance	Experienced meaningfulness of work	High quality of work performance
Autonomy	Experienced responsibility for outcomes of work	High satisfaction with work
Feedback	Knowledge of the actual results of work	Low absenteeism and turnover

Employee growth, need, strength

According to this model the psychological states, ie *experienced
meaningfulness, experienced responsibility* for the outcomes of
work and *knowledge of the results of work*, have a critical
influence on motivation, performance and job satisfaction.
This element of the model is based on the notion of personal
reward or *reinforcement* (*see* chapter 2). Reinforcement is

obtained when a person becomes aware (knowledge of results) that he or she has been responsible for (experienced responsibility) good performance on a task that he or she cares about (experienced meaningfulness).

The critical psychological states exert an influence on the outcome variables shown in the model. So that, for example, a person who was conducting a task that he or she did not care about and/or was not aware of how well they were doing would be unlikely to experience a high level of internal motivation, or to produce high quality work. How can jobs be designed so that people do experience high internal motivation and produce high quality work?

According to the theory the answer to this lies in designing job tasks so that they are high on the core job dimensions.

Skill variety: the extent to which the activities in the job call for a selection of abilities and skills (the meaning of the word variety given here differs from Cooper's use of the word described earlier in this chapter).

Task identity: the degree to which the job requires completion of a whole and identifiable piece of work.

Task significance: the extent to which the job has a substantial impact on the lives or work of other people.

Taken together these three dimensions influence the experienced meaningfulness of the work.

Autonomy: the freedom and independence that the job holder has, including discretion to schedule the work and decide upon the procedures used to carry it out. This job dimension influences the experienced responsibility for outcomes of the work and the extent to which the job holder experiences personal responsibility for the outcomes.

Feedback: the extent to which the job holder obtains direct and clear information about performance effectiveness. This core job dimension influences the results known of the work activities experienced by the job holder.

One final feature of the job characteristics model should be mentioned. This concerns the extent to which people differ in their levels of growth need. People with high growth need strength (GNS) are more likely, or able, to experience changes in their critical psychological states when core job dimensions are improved. On the part of the model this represents recognition of the fact that people are different and that people who are more concerned with self-growth and development will respond more positively to favourable core job dimensions.

Taken as a whole, the job characteristics model provides a clear prescription for the design of job tasks to maximize personal and work outcomes such as satisfaction and performance.

Evaluation of the job characteristics model

To what extent does the model provide an accurate (ie valid) view of the links between job dimensions, psychological states and outcomes? Tests of the model (Algera, 1983; Arnold and House, 1980; Champoux, 1991; Kiggundu, 1983) suggest that the core job dimensions specified in the model do indeed influence personal and work outcomes. The original model, however, proposes clearly that the critical psychological states are the 'causal core of the model' (Hackman and Oldham, 1975), ie job dimensions influence psychological states, and critical psychological states then influence the outcome variables. The limited empirical research, focusing specifically on the psychological states, has produced mixed results, casting doubt on the validity of this particular aspect of the model. For example, Kiggundu (1983) found a positive relationship between the three critical psychological states and autonomy, but a negative relationship with feedback from the job itself. Arnold and House (1980) found that task identity was not associated with any of the psychological states, while Wall et al (1978) obtained only partial support for the function of the psychological states upon any outcome variables.

In scientific terms the validity of the model is crucial. Any theoretical model is valid only if it provides a completely accurate view of the causes and effects involved. The job characteristics model may not have been proved entirely valid but, as Wall and Martin (1987) point out, the model's influence stems from its identification of a particular set of variables and the provision of instruments to measure them. 'This has given a consistency of focus . . . which other approaches have failed to achieve' (p 68).

Roberts and Glick (1981) in a comprehensive narrative review noted a number of potential problems with the model. These

65

include the fact that although many of the predicted relationships have been found, it may be the result of common method variance. For example, it has been shown that people seek to avoid inconsistencies when answering questionnaires (Salancik and Pfeffer, 1977). However, the majority of studies testing the model have used information about task characteristics, and the attitudes of task performers, from questionnaires administered to the same people. High correlations, therefore, might be expected on the basis of people's desire for cognitive consistency rather than owing to any other link between the measures involved. Algera (1983) examined this possibility and obtained significant support for the job characteristics approach when he found the relationships between task characteristics and the reactions of task performers to be quite similar, regardless of whether supervisor ratings or self-ratings were used.

Other criticisms raised the point that while the model identifies important task characteristics and their relationship to outcomes, those relationships are moderated by the influence of individual growth need strength. Roberts and Glick asserted that the model is useful only to individuals high on GNS, and that the theory makes no attempt to identify desirable task attributes for low-GNS individuals. Champoux (1991) provides some empirical support for the moderating effects of GNS. He found that high-GNS people were predicted to respond more positively to job enrichment, and that low-GNS people responded negatively to job enrichment. On the basis of these findings, Champoux suggests that the level of GNS in those who have been targeted for job enrichment programmes should be assessed, as this variable may be more crucial to success than had been previously thought.

Fried and Ferris (1987) conducted a qualitative review of the job characteristics model, utilizing meta-analytic techniques (Hunter et al, 1982) which provided support for the model in general, and the intervening effects of the critical psychological states in particular. Specifically, Fried and Ferris found that (1) the core job dimensions were strongly related to the three critical psychological states, and these psychological states were more highly related to motivation and job satisfaction outcomes than the core job dimensions. In contrast to the model's prediction, the critical psychological states were not related to performance outcomes; (2) the job feedback characteristic appears to affect all three critical psychological states;

and (3) the number of critical psychological states could be reduced from three to two by integrating experienced meaningfulness and responsibility into a single dimension. Moreover, the results suggest that the five core job dimensions may be reduced, as skill variety, task significance and autonomy might be part of one dimension. Other evidence implies that the core job dimensions may be incomplete. Wall *et al* (1990) indicate that several features of job design impact upon performance, job satisfaction and job-related stress. They identified job control, cognitive demand and social factors as key elements of the job characteristics approach.

Although highly related to autonomy, which generally means working with minimal or no supervision, job control is defined explicitly as the 'employee's opportunity and responsibility to actively influence work outcomes'. The construct of job control is central to the notion of skill (Wood, 1989) and stress (Smith, 1985). Cognitive demand is a construct that relates to the number of problem-solving, planning, diagnostic and system understanding aspects of an individual's work. At present this construct is overlooked by current theory in work design (Wall and Martin, 1987). Social interaction is a construct that reflects the fact that social factors affect job perceptions, attitudes and behaviour. It appears that these factors complement rather than invalidate the job characteristics approach (Wall and Martin, 1987).

Although there have been a number of important criticisms, the job characteristics model has generally withstood scientific testing, especially given the large number of possible correlations between the different variables. As a basis for practical job design and redesign it provides an integration of previous research findings and is one of the best contemporary approaches available. In addition to the theoretical model, the designers of the job characteristics model provide clear guidance on how to use the model as a basis for the practical redesign of jobs (see Hackman and Oldham, 1980, and chapter 5 in this book).

The job diagnostic survey

Hackman and Oldham (1975) have also developed a questionnaire: the job diagnostic survey (JDS). The JDS provides

measurements of all the major components of the job characteristics model, and its major intended uses include:

1 The diagnosis of existing jobs prior to planned work design.
2 The evaluation of the effects of work redesign activities.
  For example, to determine which job dimensions did or did
  not change.
3 The assessment of the impact of the changes on the motivation and satisfaction of employees.

For example, the questionnaire can be used to provide a
motivating potential score (MPS) for a job, derived from
scores produced for the five core job dimensions, by job
holders.

$$\text{Motivating Potential Score (MPS)} = \frac{[Skill\ variety + Task\ identity + Task\ significance]}{3} \times \text{Autonomy} \times \text{Feedback}$$

$$\text{ie MPS} = \left[\frac{SV + Tl + TS}{3}\right] \times \text{Aut} \times \text{Fee}$$

Scores on core job dimensions can range from 1 to 7. Thus a
total score of 343 is possible, although typical scores vary,
with an average of approximately 150. Fried and Ferris (1987)
indicated that the MPS, as a summary index of the individual
job characteristics, demonstrated stronger relationships with
the psychological states and work outcomes than with any of
the individual core job dimensions. Simply adding the scores
of each job characteristic, however, had the same, if not better,
predictive validity as using the multiplicative MPS index.
Moreover, on the basis of a sub-set analysis, they found that
job holders' descriptions of their jobs on the JDS correlated
highly with supervisory descriptions of the same jobs. This
implies that responses on the JDS are indicative of real aspects
of a job, and are not simply a reflection of the respondents'
attitudes and preconceptions.

Hackman and Oldham propose that the JDS should be used
as a diagnostic aid for job redesign programmes. A case study
utilizing the JDS in this way is presented in chapter 4, while
further detail on the JDS and the use of the job characteristics

model as a basis for practical job redesign is presented in chapters 4, 5 and 6.

During the decade since the development of the JDS a number of revisions have been suggested. Many of these suggestions have called for the inclusion of additional factors (Zoccaro and Stone, 1988) such as job-related danger and intellectual demand. Others, such as Campbell (1988) and Gerhart (1988), have called for better measures of key terms such as job complexity.

Socio-technical systems approaches to job design

Davis (1966) has described the process of job design as:

. . . specification of the contents, methods, and rela-tionships of jobs in order to satisfy technological and organizational requirements as well as the social and personal requirements of the job holder. (p 21).

This definition reflects an emphasis on an approach to the issues involved in job design, the social-technical systems approach (*see* chapters 1 and 3), which differs from the job characteristics approach.

Advocates of the socio-technical approach (eg Emery, 1959; Taylor, 1975; Davis, 1966) have often emphasized the role that autonomous work groups can play in job design. Emery (1959) for example argues that group tasks, if they are genuinely interdependent and provide people with true autonomy, can be more satisfying and motivating than individual work.

Emery (1980) states that:

In designing a social system to efficiently operate a modern capital intensive plant the key problem is that of creating self-managing groups to man the interface with the technical system. (p 21).

As ideas concerning job design have developed various terms have been used to refer to groups of workers who have some control over their own working procedures and production systems. Emery prefers the term 'self-managing' but other authors use terms such as 'autonomous', 'semi-autonomous' or 'relatively autonomous'. There seems to be no agreed terminology. It is however possible to attach some general meaning to the concept involved.

Essentially such a working group has responsibility for some aspects of the control of its own work. Gulowsen (1972) has identified several aspects that determine the extent to which a group may be described as autonomous (or self-managing). The group may have influence on:

individual production method
internal leadership
recruitment
internal task distribution
production method (of the group)
when to work
additional tasks
external leadership
quantitative goals
qualitative goals.

Groups may be more or less autonomous depending on which items they can influence.

As, well as emphasizing the contribution that autonomous working groups might play, socio-technical systems theorists also attempt to pay attention to the complex interactions that take place between variables at all levels within the socio-technical system (*see* figure 10). The job characteristics model by contrast focuses much more specifically on the design of job tasks and their impact on individuals and group factors (*see* figure 9, page 63).

Despite their differences the socio-technical systems

Figure 10
How to improve key job characteristics

Levels within the
socio-technical system

Socio-technical → { Individual } ← Job characterization
systems approach { Group } model
{ Department/unit
{ Total organization

approach and job characteristics model do seem to converge as far as the job characteristics that are important in individual work are concerned and both approaches identify much the same factors as being important, ie autonomy, skill variety, task identity, task significance and feedback. Socio-technical systems theorists also stress the importance of jobs providing job holders with opportunities for continuous learning.

Kemp *et al* (1983) describe the two approaches thus:

. . . the Job Characteristics Model . . . partly through being limited in focus and commendably specific in exposition, has inspired a vast body of research. In contrast, the socio-technical systems approach to work design, manifest in the notion of autonomous or self-regulating work groups . . . is much more inclusive . . . Nevertheless, lack of precision concerning salient variables and their specific interrelationships (Van de Zwann, 1975; Klein, 1979) has undermined its theoretical impact. In short, the socio-technical systems approach, despite its theoretical breadth, has not succeeded in guiding detailed empirical research towards a broader perspective. (p 273).

Important research by Campion and Thayer (1985) suggests that an interdisciplinary approach may be a more fruitful perspective to apply to job design, as no single approach can explain all outcomes. A taxonomy of job design approaches from different disciplines and a multi-method job design questionnaire to reflect the different approaches was developed. The perspectives used were the motivational approach from organizational psychology, a mechanistic approach from industrial engineering, a biological approach from work physiology and biomechanics, and a perceptual/motor approach from experimental psychology. A field study was undertaken with 23 supervisors and 215 job holders from 121 different jobs, in five manufacturing plants. The results suggested that different approaches influenced different outcomes, some of which might have some costs as well as benefits. Specifically, the results showed that those who scored high on the motivational scale were more satisfied with their jobs, more motivated, rated higher on job performance indices and exhibited less absenteeism. Those who scored high on the mechanistic scale utilized more equipment and needed less training time to learn the use of the equipment.

High scores on the biological scale showed that operators expended less physical effort on tasks, had fewer aches and pains and reported fewer medical incidents. Finally, jobs scoring high on the perceptual/motor scale were less likely to produce accidents, errors, stress or work overload, and to require less mental demands. The authors concluded that the use of the interdisciplinary approach may provide the basis for a comprehensive theory of job design that satisfies the needs both of individuals and of organizations.

Redesigning jobs

Job design theories provide a conceptual basis for the practical redesign of jobs. Hackman (1979), for example, has suggested how changes in the core job dimensions can be brought about by making various specific job changes. Some ideas for improving key job characteristics are given in figure 11. The ideas apply to either individual or group tasks and incorporate some of those proposed by Hackman (1979).

Several types of changes can be utilized when jobs are redesigned, and some of the more common changes are given below.

Job enlargement: the addition of further, often similar task(s) to a person's job.

Job enrichment: the addition of new tasks which may previously have been done at another stage of the work process or at a different level of authority.

Job rotation: the movement of individual workers (often within a group) around a variety of tasks.

Autonomous/self-managing groups: formal working groups with some degree of autonomy to determine their own working procedure and production systems.

Examples of the implementation of several of the above are given in chapter 6.

Job context characteristics

Tasks are often organized on a group basis and groups or individuals conducting tasks do so within the wider context of

72

Figure 11
Approaches to job design

To influence **skill variety**	Provide opportunities for people to do several tasks (eg job rotation) Combine tasks Establish client relationships
To influence **task identity**	Combine tasks Form natural work units eg a typist does all the work of one person, instead of the work of several people
To influence **task significance**	Form natural work units Inform people of the importance of their work Establish client relationships
To influence **autonomy**	Give people responsibility for determining their own working systems Give people responsibility for quality control
To influence **feedback**	Establish client relationships Open feedback channels

the whole organization. Context factors such as the group and the organization are of considerable importance for motivation, performance and satisfaction at work. Hackman (1980) makes several important points when discussing the relationships between groups and motivation. First, he draws a distinction between 'coacting groups' and 'work teams':

A coacting group is a set of people who have face to face contact and plenty of opportunities for informal interaction but who do not work together on a common group task . . . A work team, on the other hand, is itself an intact performing unit.

73

Hackman argues that, from the point of view of motivation and productivity, coacting groups and work teams need to be considered separately. Coacting groups are much more prevalent in the workplace than are work teams. Coacting groups can have a significant effect on the quality of a person's work life and on productivity. Hackman (1980) notes that, like all groups, coacting groups evolve norms that may influence productivity, positively or negatively. He suggests three factors that may be important in affecting the direction (ie positive or negative) of productivity norms:

(a) The motivational structure of the jobs members perform, (b) the equity and munificence of the reward system through which members are recognized and compensated for their work, and (c) the quality of the relationships between group members and their formal supervisors. Thus, when the work itself is repetitive and boring, when rewards for the work are few and inequitably distributed, and when relationships with supervisors are characterized by mutual distrust and distorted communication, then we would not be surprised to observe productivity-restricting norms develop among group members. (p 392).

As far as work teams are concerned, Hackman suggests that attention should be paid to the design of work teams rather than, as has happened in some cases, assuming that teams will work things out for themselves. He proposes that specific attention should be paid to the structure of the group task. The composition of the work team and the early creation of sound, productivity-linked group norms are also important. Tasks are often organized on a group basis when the task is too complex for an individual to perform in the required time. The complex task is broken down into smaller part-tasks which are shared among a number of individuals. A group task is defined in terms of interdependence between part-tasks and the existence of a common goal, as with a team of doctors and nurses conducting a surgical operation.

The form of interdependence and coordination in the group depends on the degree of complexity of the group task. Complexity itself is defined first in terms of predictability/unpredictability, ie variability over time, and secondly degree of similarity/dissimilarity between constituent elements of the task. In highly complex tasks, ie those that are unpredictable and consist of many dissimilar elements, interdependence tends to be reciprocal. That is, group members contribute reciprocally to each other's activities and coordination tends to be by mutual adjustment, with group members adjusting their activities on the basis of variable task demands. In less complex group tasks, interdependence tends to be sequential, that is, activities take a serial form and coordination is usually planned with rules which govern members' interdependent actions. As far as the design of group tasks is concerned, the orthodox job-design view (see Hackman, 1977) is that a group task designed to be high on the five core job dimensions of the job characteristics model would be expected to produce high task-relevant motivation. Based on his experience of group work redesign, Wall (1980) notes that, although the job characteristics model is useful as far as the design of the *task* is concerned, it does not provide a comprehensive framework encompassing all the factors relevant to the design of group work.

> Its main deficiency in practice was that it left out of account a range of contextual variables of evident significance – in particular those concerned with technology, supervisory roles and managerial practices. (p 330).

More recently, Wall (1984) has argued that the impact of job redesign on management practice and on supervision in particular has been systematically underestimated.

The workgroup, whether it is a coacting group or a work team, represents part of the wider context for many individuals at work. As the points made above suggest, there are other, more general work-context factors that must also be borne in mind in any job redesign exercise. Individual performance at work is a function of many aspects of the wider organizational environment. Steers (1979), for example, suggests four major work-context factors: managerial policies and practices, organization structure, technology, and the external environment combine to create the climate of an organization. Individual outcomes (performance, satisfaction, involvement) are then determined by the combined effects of organizational climate and employee characteristics.

Steers (1979, p 372), after reviewing work on the relationship between climate, job satisfaction and job performance concludes that:

... a picture emerges in which the most favourable climate for both production and satisfaction is generally one that emphasizes *both* employee achievement *and* employee consideration. That is, we can generally conclude that one way for managers to facilitate effectiveness is to bring about a climate that stresses the importance of goal attainment, while at the same time encouraging mutual support, cooperation and participation in the activities that contribute to goal attainment. (*See* chapter 1 for further discussion of organizational climate.)

Figure 12 indicates the main groups of work-context factors related to motivation, job satisfaction and performance at work. The relationships between some of the factors shown in figure 12 are fairly well understood and strong theoretical bases exist for developing high levels of performance. For example, the behavioural approach to motivation (*see* chapter 2) provides firm prescriptions concerning the managerial and supervisory practices that will enhance performance. The job characteristics model in this chapter suggests links between task characteristics and performance. Other relationships are less well understood. A coherent and comprehensive approach to motivation needs to pay attention to all these factors. Despite this emphasis that all the factors are impor-

Figure 12
Work-context factors related to motivation and satisfaction

Supervisory and management practices
Organizational reward system
Supervision/management style
Organizational climate
Technology and the physical environment
Organization structure
Social/group factors

tant, it is also clear that some are more central to the problem of motivation and performance than others. Furthermore, some factors are easier to influence and change than others.

When attempting to improve or maintain motivation and performance, the characteristics from figure 12 that are of primary importance will vary according to the nature of the people, jobs and the organization involved. In most circumstances, however, task characteristics, managerial and supervisory policies and social factors will be important.

Chapter 4 deals with the measurement of motivation and job satisfaction, chapter 5 with redesigning jobs to increase motivation and satisfaction; chapter 6 give examples of this in practice.

4 Measuring motivation in organizations

Many of today's organizations are so large and complex that keeping track of employees' levels of motivation is a difficult task. Traditional methods of communication are often suspect and reports are often filtered as they pass through the organization. Some managers and departmental heads simply ignore problems of motivation and morale. Others magnify problems as a lever to attract attention, gain personal status or extract extra resources for their empires. Still other managers hide problems of morale and motivation in a well meaning attempt 'to keep the lid on' the situation and prevent it from becoming worse. Amongst all the distortion, claims and counter claims, it is often impossible to separate the wheat from the chaff and identify low levels of motivation which really deserve attention and resources; until they become real problems and a crisis is only too evident.

One possible way to identify poor motivation is to undertake an organizational survey which is carefully planned and which will yield precise, quantifiable results. The fact that the results are quantified rather than expressed in vague terms such as 'many' or 'few' means that resources can be deployed with greater precision or effectiveness. The following three examples demonstrate some of the major aspects of surveys.

Three case studies of measuring organizational motivation

Case study one: a very large international company

The first case study concerns a large multinational company in which management possessed a determination to do things right. It decided that, rather than react to events, it would try to anticipate them. It embarked on a long term programme whereby it would survey its employees once every two years, with the possibility of more specific and smaller surveys in the intervening periods. It commissioned consultants who produced a questionnaire covering 13 aspects of worker satisfaction. The survey questionnaire presented formidable problems because it was to be used in seven different European countries and to ensure maximum usefulness two steps were taken. First, translations were checked via a process of 'back translation'. It was translated from English to the second language and then this version was independently translated back into English. The two English versions were compared and any discrepancies reconciled. Secondly, the questionnaire distributed by the European headquarters comprised only the core part of the questionnaire and concerned only those aspects which were relevant to direct international comparisons. The individual countries were able to add additional questions which were relevant to their interests.

A sample of almost 3,000 managerial and technical employees completed the questionnaire.

One of the major outcomes of the survey was to identify areas which did not present problems. Thus the company avoided wasting resources in an attempt to produce unnecessary improvements. For example the company found that, on a continental basis, their employees were more than happy with the pay, training and the management they had received. This latter finding came as something of a surprise to management: it appeared they had been over-sensitive to those with loud voices and gripes and they had underestimated the satisfaction of the silent majority. However, the survey also indicated considerable dissatisfaction with career development within the company. The survey results led directly to a major review and substantial changes in the career structure within the organization.

More detailed analysis revealed more specific results. For example, the results from Finland indicated dissatisfaction among technologists with their immediate boss and as a result special training courses were provided for the Finnish bosses. Similarly, detailed analysis in the UK indicated dissatisfaction with job security and training.

By themselves these results saved the company eight times

79

the actual cost of the survey. This example provides an illustration of surveys which are used as a diagnostic device. (The uses of surveys will be considered more systematically later in this chapter). The concrete results convinced the organization of the usefulness of job satisfaction surveys and the decision to undertake a company-wide survey every two years was confirmed.

The organization was able to build up a chart of the vital aspects of its employees' psychological well being in much the same way that a physician maintains a chart of a patient's physiological well being by taking readings of temperature and pulse. Such regular monitoring provided a baseline which enabled the early identification of problems. For example, over the years there was a small but steady improvement in employees' satisfaction with communications. Then, the results of one survey indicated that satisfaction with communication in its Spanish subsidiary had suddenly fallen to a low level. A small but more detailed survey among its Spanish employees was commissioned which confirmed the trend. The greater detail of the second survey allowed the problem to be pinpointed and the cause identified. Preliminary discussions had suggested the likely difficulties and questions concerning centralization, role conflict, functional specialization, upward information distortion, adequacy of horizontal communication etc were incorporated into the questionnaire. In essence, the results of the secondary survey showed that the fall in satisfaction with communications among its Spanish workforce focused upon a new, more centralized working procedure which made employees feel compelled to distort or suppress unfavourable information in the reports they were required to submit to head office. This particular incident illustrates that since the organization had used surveys over a number of years and had established a baseline, it was able to detect a problem before it manifested itself as acute symptoms of a deep seated issue. It is an example of surveys being used in a predictive way. A particularly fascinating aspect of this incident arises from the fact that the Spanish reorganization had produced pressures to distort the upward flow of communication. Consequently, if the company had relied upon the normal reporting process and the normal channels of communication, the problems caused by centralization would not have become apparent, not until they had grown into such proportions that an eruption would have become inevitable. The surveys also provided the company with another advantage. They allowed it to evaluate the effectiveness of many of its actions. For example, the first survey in the series identified dissatisfaction with immediate superiors in Finland. A management training programme was prepared and implemented by the Finnish subsidiary. The results of the second survey showed that the new training programme had achieved a large degree of success in improving employees' satisfaction with their bosses. In other situations, the surveys revealed that managerial actions had been inappropriate and had not brought about the desired change. Thus the surveys played a part in guiding the company towards policies and actions which were effective.

This example of the widespread and sophisticated use of organizational surveys demonstrates many points concerning the employment of surveys. However, their use is not restricted to large multinational companies. Surveys are also useful in medium and small organizations.

Case study two: a medium sized organization

A medium sized textile company in the North provides an interesting example of surveys used as an investigative tool. The company was involved in making up lingerie which was sold through a leading chain store. The problem at 'Sheila Works' was quite clear: massive labour turnover among the sewing machinists in the 'making up' departments. The company commissioned a job satisfaction survey to discover the cause. A questionnaire was designed which dealt with training, supervision, workplace, wages and hours and it was administered to 40 recruits, 40 leavers and 40 sewing machinists who were not leaving the company. The results were quite surprising. In spite of the high turnover the sewing machinists were very satisfied with most aspects of their job. Indeed, satisfaction increased the longer the employee had worked for the company and satisfaction amongst leavers was just as high as among those who were staying. However, the survey also revealed that the labour turnover was most frequent among young sewing machinists who were leaving not because of dissatisfaction with the company but because they were starting a family or for other personal reasons. The evidence from the survey indicated clearly that the company would be wasting its resources if it tried to increase job satisfaction further. A more effective solution was to abandon traditional prejudices against training women in their thirties and to employ older applicants who were returning to work after child rearing. This strategy was pursued and training methods were adapted to suit the needs of older trainees. Within a short period of time the problem of labour turnover ceased to exist.

Case study three: a small organization

In general, motivational surveys are less frequent in small companies. However, surveys can still have a useful role to play because they are precise, quantitative and allow comparisons with other organizations. Comparability is an important point. A manager of a small upholstery company may judge which departments or individuals pose motivational problems but cannot easily judge how the motivation in his or her departments compare with similar departments in other firms.

A typical example of a survey in a small firm is given by Deeks and Company, a company of 40 employees manufacturing electronic components in Whaley Bridge. An unacceptably high rate of returns prompted an investigation. It was clear that the problem concerned the jobs of the assemblers and the inspectors but the exact nature of the problem was far less clear. The company commissioned a small survey of its four inspectors and 20 assemblers. They used the job diagnostic survey (JDS) developed by Hackman and Oldham (1974). The JDS is a complex questionnaire which attempts to measure how motivating jobs are. It is based on an explicit model (the model is discussed fully in chapter 3.) The model maintains that a job must have three attributes if it is to have the potential for motivating employees.

The JDS allows each of these (and several other) facets of job motivation to be measured. The company asked its assemblers and inspectors to complete the questionnaire and the results are shown in figure 13.

Thus it can be seen that neither job has a particularly high motivating potential. A study by Oldham, Hackman and Stepina (1978) suggests that the average job achieves a

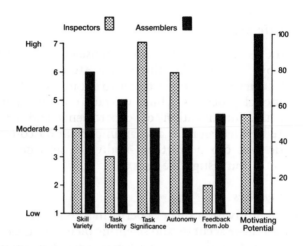

Figure 13
Analysis of two jobs using the job diagnostic survey (JDS)

motivating potential score (*see* chapter 3) of 128. The motivating potential score for Inspectors (55) and Assemblers (100) is below average and puts them in the bottom 10 per cent and 30 per cent of jobs respectively. Clearly, both jobs are uninspiring but the inspection job is particularly uninspiring. The job of inspector offers considerable freedom and its significance to the organization is clear but it is also monotonous, meaningless and gives little indication whether the job is being performed correctly. In this particular company the inspector's job was in dire need of restructuring to make it more motivating. Some techniques for doing this are considered in chapter 6.

Uses of measuring motivation in organizations

The examples of surveys in large, medium and small organizations are designed to give a quick impression of the relevance of measuring motivation to all sizes of organizations. They are case studies and whilst they demonstrate many points they should be assessed systematically under the uses that surveys have for measuring motivation at work. Three distinct uses may be identified: diagnostic uses, uses in organization development and uses in evaluation. These

83

categories are not mutually exclusive and they need to be explained in more detail.

Diagnostic uses

Diagnostic use is the most established use of surveys and it is typified by each of the three case studies. In essence, diagnostic surveys are undertaken to locate departments or organizational processes which warrant remedial action (in practice, the identification of departments and processes which are best left alone is also an important outcome). The diagnostic uses can be further subdivided into descriptive, predictive and investigative uses.

Descriptive uses

Almost all motivation surveys perform a descriptive function by giving a more accurate and scientific picture of the existing state of affairs than the picture given by anecdote, reports and pressures from special interest groups. In a large organization this is particularly useful in allowing senior management to take a 'bird's eye view' of the situation when making strategic policy decisions such as deciding whether to invest resources in additional plant or whether to invest resources in improving the satisfaction of employees. This descriptive function is enhanced by the qualitative nature of the results and, where sufficient background data exists, by precise comparisons with comparable groups in other companies.

Predictive uses

When used in a predictive way, measures of organizational motivation try to give warning of problems which are likely to arise or existing problems that are likely to become acute. The company is then able to take preventative action. As the old adage says 'prevention is better than cure' and usually prevention is far less costly. The preventative uses are demonstrated by the first case study in a large international organization. Predictive uses often entail an organization surveying its workforce on a regular basis, say every one or two years and even establishing a permanent department or section to organize the surveys.

Investigative uses

The second case study demonstrates the investigative uses. Even when the existence of a problem is quite apparent its nature and causes may be blurred and poorly distinguished. A carefully controlled, quantitative survey can permit the components of a problem to be identified and untangled. This can save considerable money: pursuing the wrong course not only wastes resources but there may be a huge opportunity cost which arises from leaving the real problem unsolved. The events at 'Sheila Works' were a classic example of this point. The company could have spent a fortune in futile attempts to improve the satisfaction of its sewing machinists and at the end of the day the turnover problem would have remained acute. By revealing the true cause of the problem as an age and training problem the survey enabled the company to target its efforts and resolve the problem in just over a year.

The diagnostic uses of surveys boil down to providing an extra channel of communication between the employer and the employee. Surveys provide management with extra information which is relevant to important aspects of employee behaviour such as turnover, absenteeism, lateness and union activity. Surveys of this kind are most useful in organizations where some of the following conditions apply:

- a high level of organizational complexity exists
- there is a dynamic, competitive environment
- the organization must adapt rapidly
- resources, especially human resources, are limited
- accurate quantifiable results are needed.

Uses in organization development (OD)

The implications of organizational surveys for OD have been appreciated only relatively recently. Yet all stages in a survey help an organization develop its capability to adapt to its environment by helping to crystallize organizational objectives, to build a common culture, to establish a climate of open communication and to develop individuals.

Defining objectives and establishing a common culture
The planning stages of a survey inevitably involve defining the survey's objectives. This process usually has a wider effect and

85

helps the organization clarify and crystallize many of its aims. Similarly, surveys will involve a wide range of people who find participation an informative experience. The questions can provoke thought about issues they had previously taken for granted. Furthermore, a survey is an experience shared by a substantial proportion of employees. The sharing can play a part in building a 'common culture' that can help bind an organization together and can help increase group cohesiveness.

Establishing a climate of open communication

One of the most significant impacts of surveys on organizational development is the effect on company communication. By their very nature, surveys provide improved upward communication. Less obviously surveys can also stimulate downward communication. Summaries of the results are usually disseminated and in many cases feedback sessions are organized to discuss the results with participants. The meetings give an overt demonstration of the company's interest in more open communications which can then be formalized as company policy.

Developing individuals

Some surveys involve managers interviewing employees from other units. The experience provides a broadening of the managers' knowledge and provides in-depth insights which are almost impossible to obtain by any other method of management training. Practically all managers who take part in this kind of survey report that it is fascinating and very worthwhile (Smith and Dunham, 1979).

In many cases, it is possible to give managers feedback of the results obtained from their own subordinates. Obviously, in very small units, care should be taken to ensure confidentiality. However, the provision of hard quantitative data on the views of subordinates together with data which enables direct comparisons with how other groups view their boss can be a crucial factor in the personal development of many managers. Indeed, Bowers (1973) suggests that surveys are possibly the most effective technique of organizational development. He compared five different techniques of organizational development.

Survey feedback methods: produced the greatest changes both in individuals and in organizations. These methods obtained desirable changes in 23 out of the 36 measures used in the study.

Interpersonal process consultation: a technique which aims to develop a group's ability to form and implement its own change programme. Typically, a change agent gains the trust of a group and acts as a catalyst who exposes attitudes, feelings and conflicts which are often repressed. This technique produced seven desirable changes.

Data handback: involves merely returning the survey results to managers without any explanation or interpretation. Data handback resulted in nine desirable changes and three undesirable changes.

Task and process consultation: typically involve a change agent who analyses the task facing a group and attempts to identify objectives, potential resources and obstacles. This technique of organizational development produced two desirable and five undesirable organizational changes.

Laboratory training: sometimes called 'team development training' or 'T Group' training seemed to be counter-productive. It produced 13 undesirable changes and only three desirable changes.

Bowers' work and conclusions involve a number of important methodological issues and a reading of the original paper is highly recommended. However, his results clearly indicate that surveys and survey feedback can be a powerful tool for developing an organization.

Uses in evaluation

The usefulness of measuring organizational motivation, in terms of evaluating the effectiveness of managerial actions, is fairly self-evident and is also illustrated by the first case study involving a large international company. For example, the Finnish subsidiary was able to use the results from the second survey to evaluate the effectiveness of the management training programme which was instigated in order to eradicate the negative reactions towards management which were revealed in the first survey.

The evaluative potential is even more pronounced when organizations include abstract objectives such as providing employees with an acceptable quality of working life, high job satisfaction or low levels of stress which do not cause physical or psychological damage. In these circumstances, surveys of organizational motivation and morale are, perhaps, the only way of gauging the effectiveness of policies and their implementation.

Financial implications of measuring motivation

The financial impact of the diagnostic, OD and evaluative functions of surveys can be major and have considerable financial implications. Likert (1961) pioneered the technique of *human resource accounting* which attempts to monitor the valuable resource of employees' motivations etc in the same way that traditional accounting attempts to monitor a company's financial resources. Probably the best example of this approach is Mirvis and Lawler's (1977) evaluation of the financial impact of job satisfaction and attitudes in terms of absenteeism, turnover and performance. The study involved bank tellers and the results indicate that using surveys to improve the motivation of bank tellers by a small amount (1/12th of the total range) would lead to direct savings of $17,664 and a potential cost saving of $125,160 per year. The saving per teller was estimated to be $782 per year.

Another example of the benefits of improving satisfaction is given by Smith and Dunham (1979). The Hanover Radio Company employed 375 workers to assemble portable transistor radios. In response to the high cost of returns and warranty work the President of the company took the step of writing to each employee telling them that poor work standards and low performance could be tolerated no longer. He went on to say that unless there was an improvement 10 per cent of workers would be laid off. After the receipt of the letter, performance of workers fell a further 20 per cent. In response to this, the President sent another letter and imposed a wage reduction of 10 per cent until productivity improved. Within two weeks 45 of the workers quit and there was a massive increase in union membership. Smith and Dunham conclude that while the normal observational techniques had produced accurate information about low quality radios and decreases in productivity, the company had greatly misunderstood the state of morale among its employees. This misunderstanding, which could have been detected by even the simplest survey led the company to take actions which made the situation worse.

Practical aspects of measuring motivation

The practical aspects of measuring motivation within an organization can be grouped under five headings: preparation, questionnaires, data collection, analysis and feedback.

Preparation

The crucial step in preparing a survey to measure motivation in an organization is to *define the objectives*. There should be a written statement giving the reasons for the survey and the results to be obtained. Clarity at this stage is essential. So is 'political' support. Senior management should be approached for support and their comments requested and incorporated in the statement of objectives. In most cases it is also desirable to involve worker representatives who are usually able to offer constructive advice and at a later stage play a role in encouraging employees to give their whole-hearted co-operation. However, the involvement of worker representatives sometimes requires considerable care. Sometimes a hostile reaction is produced on the basis that 'the union is the correct channel to inform management about the motivation of employees'. Sometimes an over-enthusiastic reaction is produced on the assumption that the results might be used to improve a bargaining position. The latter reaction might involve protracted discussions on the exact wording of questions and the construction of the sample which would delay actual measurement and might also jeopardize the scientific merit of the project. Clearly, the decision on whether to involve worker representation needs to be taken in the light of the circumstances of particular organizations. Once the objectives have been established arrangements can proceed to design and plan the project taking timing carefully into account. Surveys to measure motivation in organizations are most effective when they are a part of a properly constructed long term plan: it eliminates the need for crisis intervention and it ensures that departments are polled on a logical and systematic basis. The exact timing needs to be chosen with care so that times of peak activity (eg end of financial year), holidays and periods of union negotiation are avoided.

Figure 14
Graph for determining sample size

The timing of a survey may need to take the target sample into account. There are so many factors influencing the choice of sample that the following suggestions cover only the main points. The first issue concerns the size of the sample. Under most circumstances the general rule is the larger the sample the better. Statisticians such as Krejcie and Morgan (1970) provide tables for determining the sample size which might be useful for large organizations. Figure 14 is derived from the tables they use. The size of the group to be surveyed is determined and the appropriate sample size is read. For example, a factory with 2,000 employees would require a sample of 322 while a factory with 500 employees would require a sample of 217 and a small firm with only 50 employees would require a sample of 44. The graph is a very useful guide but it only offers a general rule of thumb. It makes certain (common) assumptions about the margin of error that can be tolerated. Real enthusiasts will work out the required sample size from standard texts such as Moser and Kalton (1971) or Cochran (1963).

Usually, however, strict statistical considerations are often overridden by practical constraints. For example, most organizations would prefer to distribute a questionnaire to every employee rather than, say, two out of every three employees. A complete census of this kind avoids difficulties of justifying the selection of respondents and, since most of the costs are set-up cost and overheads, the distribution and analysis of a few extra questionnaires is relatively inexpensive.

In other situations, the sampling fraction will be decided on a rationale such as 'if we use a sample of $\frac{1}{3}$ and repeat the survey every year it will be three years before anyone is questioned twice'. There is, however, one golden rule which involves looking ahead to the analysis stage and deciding upon the subanalyses that will be needed. Under most circumstances, the sample should be large enough to ensure that the sample of any subgroup of interest should not be allowed to fall below 30. For example, an organization of 3,000 employees would find that in general it would need a sample of 341, ie about 11 per cent of workers. If, however, it was particularly interested in the motivation of the 170 women supervisors in the North East, it could expect to obtain 19 respondents in this category. A sample of 19 is too small to permit the usual checks and statistical tests. In this case the company would need to decide whether to increase its sample size generally or take a bigger sample of the category of employees where there was a special interest. In situations where there are less than 30 in the category of interest, then all these employees should be included in the sample. When considering the nature of the sample, part-time employees or outworkers must not be overlooked. Often these workers can represent 30–50 per cent of employees but since their motives may be significantly different to those of full-time employees their answers should be analysed separately.

Questionnaires

There is a fundamental choice whether organizations should develop their own questionnaires or whether they should use 'off the peg' questionnaires. Almost always the preference will be for off the peg questionnaires. The reason for this preference is quite clear: it is quicker and cheaper to use existing questionnaires. Usually the designers of off the peg questionnaires will have devoted more resources to the development of a questionnaire than a typical 'in house' study can provide. Off the peg questionnaires have a further advantage: the chances are that background data already exist. The background data will mean that the interpretation of the results will be easier and richer because direct comparisons can be made with results from other organizations.

However, using an off the peg questionnaire is not without disadvantages. One of the main disadvantages is locating the questionnaire which is most relevant to the objectives of the survey. Finding the right questionnaire can involve the tedious time-consuming activity of combing a wide range of learned journals and books. The process can be almost as time consuming as constructing a questionnaire 'de nouveau'. Fortunately, the task can be reduced by referring to compendia such as Smith *et al* (1984, 1984a), Cook *et al* (1981) and Price (1972). By using these compendia it should be possible to locate relevant scales fairly quickly. A list of areas commonly measured in motivational surveys is given in figure 15.

When measuring employee motivation it is important not to rely on individual questions but to choose a scale containing several questions measuring the same aspect. Scales almost always give more accurate results since they allow random factors contained in questions to cancel each other out.

Often a search through the compendia will reveal several scales which purport to measure the same aspects of motivation such as pay. In these situations it will be necessary to choose among the contenders according to their psychometric properties of reliability and validity. Reliability can be thought of as a scale's ability to give consistent results and it is usually measured as a correlation coefficient. In general, scales with reliabilities below 0.7 should not be used. There is a general rule which links a scale's reliability with the number of questions. The more questions it contains, the more reliable the test will be. In practice, very long scales are avoided because they take up too much time. For example, measuring 10 aspects of motivation each of which uses a 20

Figure 15
Motivators commonly surveyed

1 EXTRINSIC SATISFIERS

global extrinsic satisfaction

specific extrinsic satisfiers:

pay
promotion
supervision
co-workers
other levels of workers
satisfaction with the firm
physical conditions
job security
social status
the work itself.

2 INTRINSIC SATISFIERS

global intrinsic satisfaction

specific intrinsic satisfiers:

variety of work
autonomy and freedom
responsibility
task identity
task significance.

3 MISCELLANEOUS

work involvement or alienation
ability utilization
anxiety
life satisfaction
achievement motivation.

item scale will produce a final questionnaire with 200 questions. For most satisfiers, reliable scales can be found which have between five and 10 questions. Generally, it is too risky to use scales with fewer than five questions because individual questions start to carry too much weight.

Validity of questionnaires

Validity can be thought of as a scale's ability to measure what it is supposed to measure. The first consideration is face validity, ie will the scale be suitable for the particular sample in question: does it use examples which are inappropriate, does it use difficult vocabulary etc? Face validity is not true validity in a technical sense but it is very important in gaining the co-operation of the sample. A scale with poor face validity is likely to lead to a poor response rate. Construct validity concerns the meanings and interpretations which can be drawn from the scores and this is much more difficult to establish. In the past, orthodox wisdom maintained that validity is specific to a given situation and needs to be established afresh for each use and location. However work by Schmidt *et al* (1976) indicates that validity can be generalized from one situation to another and thus the results obtained by others can be used as a guide. Validity is also generally reported in terms of a correlation coefficient. Ideally, a scale should have a validity coefficient of 0.4 or higher and a validity coefficient lower than 0.3 would only be acceptable in exceptional circumstances.

Other factors to take into account when choosing among scales are:

the ease of scoring
the availability of background data, especially norms which can be used as a standard of comparison
the availability of the scale, eg are there any copyright restrictions?

Many collections of scales exist. For example, the job descriptive index (JDI) by Smith *et al* (1969) contains 72 questions measuring satisfaction with work, supervision, promotion, co-workers and pay. Cross's (1973) worker opinion survey contains scales measuring satisfaction with pay, promotion, immediate superior, people you work with, the firm and the job itself. If the aims of the survey are met by the particular combination of motivators measured in a particular collection of scales then the collection can be adopted, lock, stock and barrel. However, this is frequently not the case and it will be necessary to choose some scales from one collection and some scales from another. Generally there is little harm in mixing scales in this way in order to achieve the survey's objectives. However, it is usually disastrous to mix questions from different scales or to alter the wording of specific questions. Mixing of questions or amending their wording usually destroys all chance of comparing results with those obtained by others. Furthermore there are some circumstances where it is better not to mix even the scales themselves. The main example here is the job diagnostic survey (JDS) by Hackman and Oldham (1976). If the JDS is used in its entirety it is possible to combine the scores from the separate scales to produce a global index of a job's motivation potential score (MPS).

The scope of motivation surveys will often be widened to include scales which are not specifically related to job satisfaction. These additional scales are included to provide a context for the results which will emerge. The additional scales are usually concerned with measuring the organization and the organizational climate. A list of additional areas is given in figure 16.

Finally, the questionnaire will include a few questions concerning the job title, department of work, length of service and other items which will be useful at the analysis stage. In most situations the final questionnaire will have fewer than 150 questions and it will be designed in a way which will make computer analysis as easy as possible.

Figure 16
Measures of organizational characteristics often included in surveys

1 MEASURES OF ORGANIZATIONAL CONTEXT
    diversity of the organization
    mechanization of the organization
    uncertainty of the environment.

2 ORGANIZATIONAL STRUCTURE
    complexity
    professionalization
    functional specialization
    functional dispersion
    role variety
    role conflict
    role ambiguity
    routinization

formalization
centralization.

3 ORGANIZATIONAL PROCESSES
administrative efficiency
planning:
future orientation
adaptability
organizing:
goal setting
performance to goals
violations in chain of command
conflict in directions
job pressure
leading and managing
communications
motivating staff
interactions between staff
decision making:
decision delay
levels of decision making
participation in decision making
control:
tolerance of error
rule observation.

4 THE PHYSICAL ENVIRONMENT

5 ORGANIZATIONAL VALUES
values concerning people
values concerning innovation and risk
values concerning ideas and research
values concerning rules
values concerning work.

Data collection

The administration of a questionnaire needs careful planning
which in the case of a large survey needs to start a year in
advance. Often meetings are arranged to explain the purposes
and the methods and to answer questions such as:

why are we doing the survey?
why are we doing the survey now?
who will see the results?

why were we selected?
will my answers be confidential?

The meeting needs to be handled with care and the questions answered openly and frankly.

Arrangements also need to be made for the distribution and collection of the questionnaires. A mechanism needs to be devised which gives the sample confidence that their replies are confidential and that they can answer frankly and openly. Often they are particularly concerned whether their immediate boss will see their completed form. One of the best ways of achieving this confidence is for employees to mail their forms independently to an outside survey organization. Alternatively, it can be arranged for a 'neutral' person to collect the questionnaires. A large survey will need a professional approach to administration which uses flow charts and progress chasers to ensure that the stages are completed to time.

Analysis

The analysis will depend upon the size of the sample and the objective of the motivation survey. If there are more than 30 questions or the sample is greater than 50, computer analysis is highly recommended. Of the main computer packages, SPSS, the Statistical Package for the Social Sciences (Nie *et al*, 1975) is probably the most suited to this type of work. An understanding of SPSS is not strictly necessary since the computing aspects can be delegated to specialists. However, it is necessary to know what analyses should be requested.

It is best to start by looking at the scores on individual scales. First, the global analysis for the entire sample should be produced. For example, if Smith's (1969) Job Descriptive Index (JDI) had been used with a sample of 400 employees, the first step would be to calculate the mean satisfaction score for satisfaction for each of the five scales (work, supervision, promotion, co-workers and pay). It might also be useful to look at the spread of scores for each scale too. Statistics, such as the mean and the range, are called descriptive statistics. SPSS produces many different descriptive statistics but in most circumstances the mean, an index of spread such as the standard deviation, and percentages are all that is required.

Figure 17

Diagram of a set of satisfaction scores from the JDI

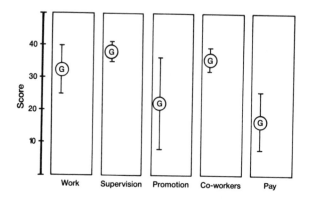

Figure 17a

Diagram of satisfaction scores from JDI with scores of individual
departments superimposed

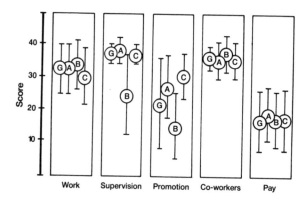

Usually, it is better to represent the results graphically as in figures 17 and 17a. From figure 17 it can be appreciated immediately that satisfaction with supervision and co-workers is high and, from the width of the bars, which indicate the spread, there is relatively little disagreement between opinions. On the other hand, the satisfaction with promotion and pay is low but there is a wider spread of opinion in these areas.

Once the global results are seen (G, in figure 17), it is then possible to obtain descriptive statistics for subgroups. In this example, employees were drawn from three departments A, B and C. The mean and spread for each department are calculated and can be superimposed on the chart. Immediately it can be seen that the problem department is department B where satisfaction with supervision and promotion is very low. The subdivision can proceed to obtain very precise results. In the present example, the results from department B were further subdivided by age and then by sex. It was found that dissatisfaction with both supervision and promotion was concentrated among male operatives in department B who were aged 25–35 years old. Armed with this information the company was able to take remedial action which was relatively inexpensive.

A slightly more complex way of looking at the results is to refer to norm tables which relate specific results to a general standard. This gives much greater insight. For example, figure 17a shows that the sample is satisfied with the supervision it receives but why is this so? There are two possible reasons. The company has good supervisors or people in general are satisfied with supervision. The two conclusions have very different sets of implications and it is important to know which is the most accurate. This can only be settled by reference to a set of norms. Not all scales have these norms, but since the JDI has been well researched norm tables are available. Indeed, they show that people are generally satisfied with supervision. Compared with this relatively high level of satisfaction in general, employees in this sample are dissatisfied with their supervisors and the score is 20 per cent below average!

Under most circumstances an examination of the descriptive statistics is all that is required. But, when the motivation survey is undertaken for diagnostic or research purposes, more complex analyses may be necessary. Relationships between two scales can be explored with the aid of cross tabulations or correlations. Still more complex statistics such as factor analysis or multiple correlations can be used to explore simultaneously the relationships between many scales (*see* Nie *et al*, 1975).

Feedback

Smith and Dunham (1979) draw attention to the fact that the results of a motivation survey need to be reported at different levels and Cameron (1973) points out that there is no fixed order in which the levels are approached.

A simultaneous approach

A simultaneous approach to all groups is often both impractical and undesirable. The findings are given the aura of 'flavour of the week' and there are reduced opportunities for discussion as the information flows from group to group. The simultaneous approach, however, seems more egalitarian than other methods.

A build-up approach

A build-up approach, in which the results are first given at supervisor level and then to management, has a number of attractions. It allows the conclusions to be tested at grass roots level before important policy decisions are made and it enables the survey team to gain experience of these meetings before they are required to present the results at senior levels.

Waterfall or cascade strategy

One of the most accepted designs is the waterfall or cascade strategy. Here the results are first given to the most senior level in the organization. Feedback is given to the next level down when it has been reasonably assimilated at the higher levels. For example, the divisional executives will first be given results showing the global results and the results of their division. When, perhaps with the aid of a change agent, the divisional results have been assimilated, each divisional executive will call a meeting of plant managers to discuss results at the different plants. The plant managers then call meetings of shift managers who discuss results for the different shifts and so on. The waterfall strategy has the advantage that supervisors of a given group have already had experience of the results before discussion with the group they supervise.

Of course, there is no reason why several strategies cannot be adopted simultaneously. Indeed, Bowers and Franklin (1977) suggest that the optimal strategy involves a waterfall design which is supplemented by almost simultaneous feedback to other levels.

Whatever method of feedback is adopted three golden rules should be observed. First, equivalent information should be given to all levels. Whilst the format and method of presentation should be modified according to the characteristics of the recipients, the information given in employee reports should, in matters of material fact, be the same as the information contained in reports to management. There should be no question of doctoring certain results. Secondly, immediate but approximate results are more effective than delayed results which are accurate to the twelfth decimal place. Although those involved in the survey may have a strong predisposition to accuracy it is a tendency which should be resisted.

The final point is a very apposite end for this section. The results and any discussion of the results should focus on the changes which can and should be made rather than looking backwards and apportioning blame. This is important because the major objective of measuring motivation in organizations is to bring about beneficial changes. Unless such changes occur, the exercise will have been a waste of time and a managerial opportunity will have been missed.

5 Job and work design as planned change

A decade ago, judging by the reports in the serious press and the informal talk among professionals in the field, it might have seemed that redesigning jobs to improve their motivational appeal was of the highest importance. Since that time the theoretical basis of the job redesign movement has come under criticism and some negative findings have emerged. Nevertheless, even by today's more sceptical standards, redesigning jobs to bring about higher levels of employee motivation is an important management strategy which can produce valuable results and make life more satisfying.

The rationale of job design

Job design arises from the fact that people do not perform the same set of tasks in any organization. The tasks are grouped in some way into jobs. The way this grouping occurs is influenced by many factors such as tradition, efficiency, the organizational power structure or chance. The important points to note are that not all of these factors are logical and the grouping is rarely made with the motivation of workers in mind. It follows that some jobs are therefore unnecessarily demotivating. As a consequence, the quality of working life is degraded and production is diminished.

It follows that in many situations, it should be possible to regroup and rearrange the tasks to make jobs better. As shown in previous chapters, researchers on industrial motivation such as Herzberg (1968), Turner and Lawrence (1965), and Hackman and Oldham (1974) suggest that motivating jobs require the exercise of a *variety of skills*, producing a *meaningful unit of work* (rather than repetitively performing a miniscule and relatively unimportant action) and having the *autonomy* to decide how the work is done, coupled with the provision of *clear* and *accurate feedback* to let job holders know how they are doing. In theory, it might be possible to redesign jobs so that they include all of these factors but in practice there are many limitations.

Four main contextual influences on job design

There are four main contextual influences on job design: the job itself, the technology, management attitudes and employee and union attitudes.

The job itself

Many jobs are inherently predictable and well defined and the scope for redesign is limited. For example, ticket office staff operate in much the same way throughout the world: they pronounce the fee, collect money from the customer, perhaps give change and then issue the ticket before dealing with the next customer. Jobs of this kind are highly programmed and it is difficult to imagine how else they could be performed. Highly programmed jobs are narrow in function and limited in content. As Cooper (1974) indicates, 'they require little or no recurrent planning and, since there is little intrinsic variance in the task, little control. They are characteristically executive in function and tend to be limited in variety, discretion and contribution'.

These jobs pose obvious problems for job redesign since they have little potential for adding functions other than executive ones. Probably the only way of redesigning jobs which have such limitations in themselves, is either to abolish or automate them.

The technology

Technology also influences the form of job design. This is perhaps best demonstrated by Woodward (1958). She looked at span of control in three different types of technology:

1 mass production organizations which essentially used production lines to manufacture cars, washing machines etc

2 small batch organizations which produced specialized products or services in small numbers, eg road transport, some consultancy type work and teaching

3 continuous process organizations which included glass making, steel making, oil refining etc.

Woodward found that the span of control varied according to the technology involved. With the technology of mass production the median span of control was between 41 and 50. In small batch production the median span of control was between 21 and 30 while in continuous process the span of control was between 11 and 20. The reasons for these findings are open to speculation. For example, Dubin (1965) suggests that part of the reason for small spans of control in process technologies is the high cost of a mistake. Under these circumstances much of the responsibility for quality control is taken from operatives and given to first line managers. Because the first line managers have these extra tasks to perform, they are unable to supervise such large numbers. Whether or not this explanation is true, the essential point remains; the technology of the organization places constraints upon the way that jobs can be designed. This conclusion is given additional support by the work of Thompson (1967), and Mahoney and Frost (1974) (see also chapter 1).

The 'information technology' revolution of the previous two decades has considerably influenced features of job design in the manufacturing and service industries. In the case of manufacturing applications, the implementation of new technology has polarized jobs with regard to the dimensions central to work design theory. Some applications have led to more simplified and repetitive jobs, while other applications require operators to take much more responsibility for machine operations and product quality (Wall and Martin, 1987). This has created a debate as to whether or not new technology entails deskilling or enskilling the workforce (see the review by Wall and Davids, 1992). Essentially, the argument for deskilling is based on scientific management assumptions (Taylor, 1911) that existing jobs can be simplified and productivity increased by incorporating operators' knowledge and skills into computer programmes. The previous operators may serve the machines by loading materials and unloading the finished products. When machines malfunction, specialists such as computer programmers, tool setters, etc, can be called upon. Thus deskilling involves a significant decrease in task variety, feedback, autonomy and other relevant job characteristics. Conversely, the argument for enskilling is based on the fact that advanced manufacturing technology is not totally reliable and is prone to frequent operational problems. Thus the training of operators to rectify these faults reduces production 'down time'. This approach is in line with current job design theory, as task variety, feedback and autonomy are increased.

The debate has prompted much research. Wall et al (1990b) investigated both sides of the argument in a study conducted in an electronics company, manufacturing printed circuit boards (an interesting irony). Prior to job redesign, the performance levels achieved over 10 working weeks by deskilled operators were recorded, and compared with 10 weeks' performance levels after job redesign procedures had enskilled the same workforce. The results demonstrated a 40 per cent decrease in 'down time' periods after enskilling. One year later the gains were still apparent (Wall and Davids, 1992), with significant labour cost savings being reported, due to fewer demands being made upon specialist staff. Moreover, the enskilled operators experienced an increase in job satisfaction but decreases in job pressures and stress effects. The authors concluded that, when new technology is characterized by technological uncertainty, enskilling rather than deskilling is the better job design strategy.

Management attitudes

Management attitudes, values and styles also determine job design. For example, management views favouring specialization and reliability will tend to produce jobs designed on the production line approach. Also a traditional, practical way of thinking will favour the evolution of job designs along traditional lines and the likelihood of introducing new methods will be small.

Employee and union attitudes

Union and employee attitudes are further relevant factors. Cooper (1974) notes, 'Problems of inter-job demarcations can severely limit job design. Even where employees can see that enlargement promises a more satisfying work experience, they may withhold or limit their commitment'. And he quotes Paul and Robertson's (1970) study in ICI where great difficulty in enlarging the jobs of process operatives was encountered. Included among other changes was the suggestion that each operator should be responsible for two specific plant efficiencies. At that time, however, there were bad feelings due to differences of opinion about holidays. In this context the proposed enrichment was interpreted by the men as the imposition of extra chores rather than an attempt to achieve job design that would be more motivating.

Different types of job enrichment

Because the limiting factors impose different constraints, different types of job enrichment are needed. The three main types are job rotation, job enlargement and autonomous working groups (AWGs).

Job rotation

Job rotation is probably the most rudimentary type of job redesign. At its simplest it involves bringing together four or five monotonous, and usually unskilled, jobs. A working schedule is drawn up in which each employee spends a limited period on each job before moving onto another. For example, in many swimming pools there are three jobs: poolside duties, locker room duties and cash desk duties. Each of the duties is unexciting and not particularly motivating. A common solution to the problem is to produce a rota in which employees spend a short time on one set of duties before moving onto another. In this way additional variety can be built into each employee's work. The simplicity of job rotation is its main advantage, little retooling or restructuring is necessary. The main disadvantages are the very limited amount of change which is achieved and that job rotation schemes may produce bickering at the change-over points where the incoming employee complains that the last person in the duty has left the work station in a mess or the job to be completed unfinished.

106

Job enlargement

Job enlargement involves widening the job to bring in additional skills and allows employees to complete a whole job, or a much larger part of a job, so that work no longer consists of short-cycle operations whose contribution to the final product seems indistinct and remote. In this way, a sense of achievement and the pride of the craftsman can be used as motivational forces. The main disadvantages of job enlargement are the likely abandonment of traditional equipment such as the conveyor belt system. Job enrichment usually involves flexible working methods which are not consistent with highly standardized conveyor belt methods. But in many instances the conveyor belt methods are highly efficient and the cost of developing alternative systems can be quite high. For example, when Volvo enriched the jobs of some of its auto workers it had to bear the cost of developing a system of pallets which could move work around the factory at a varying pace.

Autonomous working groups

Autonomous working groups carry job enrichment to its logical conclusion. Not only is the job enlarged to include a wider range of operative skills but it is also enlarged by giving employees responsibility for basic management activities, such as deciding upon the methods of work and the scheduling and planning of work. In many situations this can be achieved by individuals. The realities of commercial and manufacturing life mean that the unit of work becomes a small work group of about six employees who schedule, plan and execute complete assemblies or whole units of work (*see* chapter 6).

Job and work design as planned change

The details of job design are best described using specific case studies and several from different countries are given in the next chapter. However, the topic of job design must be seen in context as a method of achieving organizational change. Successful implementation will depend upon using an appropriate strategy for organizational change.

However well intentioned and technically accomplished the

job redesign, it needs to be introduced with care rather than being introduced by fiat.

Some practitioners have developed approaches which are specifically related to changes involving job design. Hengen (1978) is a fairly typical example.

Like Lewin (1951), Hengen's first stage concerns stability and he notes that it seems to be human nature to seek stability in order to avoid situations that upset the *status quo* and produce uncertainty.

However, inevitable changes in our environment mean that normal relationships and expectations become disrupted. The disruption can arise from technological changes, changes by competitors, social changes, changes in expectations and indeed many other sources. In terms of job design a very potent disruption is new technology.

Disruptions produce feelings of uncertainty and anxiety. The members of the organization wonder what direction the change will take and how it will affect them. Because these questions often remain unanswered, the level of anxiety increases.

The way the organization reacts to this anxiety is of crucial importance and can take three main routes. The organization can metaphorically lose its head, do something daft and then crash. Fortunately instances of this route being chosen are very rare. Alternatively, the organization can choose the ostrich strategy, stick its head in the sand and deny the need for change. The ostrich strategy has a number of advantages. It temporarily reduces anxiety and it produces greater stability. Hengen says this may seem ridiculous but it is a response that is typically used even in organizations staffed by mature and educated adults. An organization may convince itself that there is no need for alarm. However, ignoring what is really happening within does not remove the disruption. The problem continues to cause uncertainty and anxiety. Once committed to a pretence that things have not changed the charade often has to be continued. The ostrich strategy can therefore lead to a circular response where the organization begins to move faster and faster round the loop until something within the organization gives way. The third method of dealing with the anxiety is to face up to the disruptive force and try to achieve a successful solution.

Unfortunately, facing up to a disruptive force can increase

the feelings of anxiety. Decisions will have to be taken. Often the decisions will involve unfamiliar issues and they may be taken under difficult circumstances. Inevitably, uncertainty of this kind increases rather than decreases anxiety.

Once decisions concerning job design have been made, an action plan needs to be generated. All the stages of the change need to be identified and scheduled in the most effective order. At this stage, specialists such as industrial engineers, personnel managers and change agents may be involved. One strategy is to form a small steering group with responsibility for producing an action plan. A typical steering group would include the senior works manager as chairman, his senior operational managers and the senior works union representative. The main purpose of the steering group is to approve and co-ordinate detailed decisions made by several development groups. The development groups are used as a second tier operating at a detailed, departmental level. Often, the development groups consist of the departmental manager as chairman and shift engineers, foremen, quality control, production control, engineering officers, and union representatives. A detailed description of the work of the development groups will be described more fully later in the chapter.

The steering group dissolves the development groups when detailed action plans have been produced and reconstitutes them in the form of implementation groups which stimulate, co-ordinate and monitor the implementation.

The culmination of all these phases results in reorganization and changed roles. Although most job design programmes do not involve all members of an organization directly, the support and commitment of all employees is an important ingredient for success. If this ingredient is missing the change effort will deteriorate and the original situation together with the original disturbances will reassert themselves.

If however the change is successful, the new job designs become established and stability returns to the organization. These changes are depicted schematically in figure 18.

The model in the diagram sets out the main organizational aspects of implementing a work design programme. But in practice, a more detailed approach is needed once the change is implemented. An excellent model widely used is based on the work of Lewin.

109

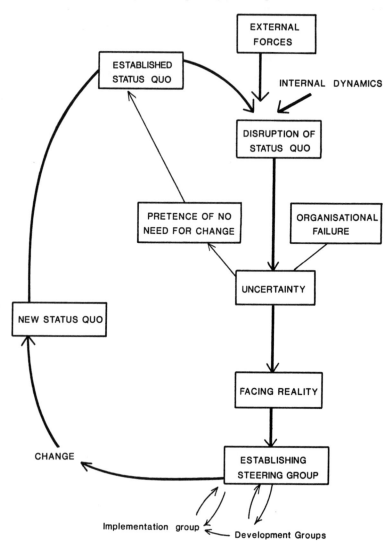

Figure 18
A systems diagram of job design

Lewin's model for change

Lewin's (1951) paradigm of change is very well known. In essence, he saw an organization as a field of social forces. Generally, these forces such as training, roles, norms and expectations act to produce stability and ensure that the organization's work continues as at the present time. Therefore, for Lewin, the first stage in introducing any significant change such as a job redesign programme is to *unfreeze* the present situation and in some way break down the existing field of forces. Unfreezing the present situation is very difficult unless some members of the organization feel the need for change and there is a new force (eg new technology) which intrudes on the system. Once the present field is unfrozen, the next phase is to *change* the field of forces in some way. In the context of this book, the change will involve some improvement in job design. The third stage of *refreezing* can bring difficulties. The refreezing can revert to the old situation so that no actual change is accomplished in the long term. More problematic is the possibility that the refreezing takes place at the wrong time and place so that only partial change, or even worse, the wrong change is implemented. Hopefully, however, the refreezing takes place at the right point and the new field of social forces acts in a way which reinforces and perpetuates the required change in jobs.

Adaptations to Lewin's model

Several authors such as Hengen (1978), Herzberg (1968), Carby (1976) and Ford (1969) have made adaptations to Lewin's approach in order to make it applicable in detail to job redesign (*see also* Hackman and Oldham, 1980). The following presents a pot pourri of their advice.

1 Developing the need for change

Some recognition of the need for change will arise directly from a decision to face reality and acknowledge that some influence which is 'disturbing' the organization must be accommodated. At this stage the feelings are ill defined and often felt by individuals who believe that the feelings are unique to themselves. Consequently, there is a reluctance to communicate these needs to others and, because the sentiments are kept private, the extent of the need is difficult to gauge. Thus at this stage one of the main priorities is to encourage individuals to talk about their views and to build up a consensus belief that a problem exists and must be tackled. It may be difficult for top management to achieve this objective

111

since they may believe that these individuals have their own axe to grind. External change agents have a distinct advantage in this respect. If an external change agent is used, then it is important to define the relationship between the organization and the agent, to assess his experience and skills, and the time he can commit to the project. Often the change agent will be able to outline alternative ways of proceeding. It is worth spending time and trouble agreeing on the kind and degree of support which each side must bring to the relationship (Hengen, 1978).

2 Clarifying and diagnosing the change

The diagnosis and classification are important and need care. If a poor solution is accepted at this stage, the whole project can proceed on the wrong basis. All assumptions should be suspended until the problem has been looked at closely. This diagnostic stage may well involve some kind of motivational survey and equally frequently it may result in a broader interpretation of the issues.

Cooper (1974) notes that selecting a site for change at this stage is an important decision. An ideal site would meet the following requirements:

(i) The chosen jobs should be likely to have a real impact on the organization's effectiveness, ie they should be jobs that contribute directly to key operational goals rather than jobs which are mainly supportive in function (eg catering, security). This is likely to produce greater credibility and helps free key managerial functions from day to day responsibilities and allows management to spend more time on long term planning.

(ii) Management and employees should be highly committed to the change. Management commitment is particularly crucial since it is inevitable that temporary setbacks will occur. Without management commitment such minor problems can cause the project to fail.

(iii) The new values and behaviour to be brought about by job design should be congruent with the values and behaviour in other parts of the organization. This is especially true for the values of other parts of the organization which have direct dealings with the chosen site.

3 Generating ideas for changing the job

Whilst the change is co-ordinated by a steering group, much of the detailed work is undertaken by development groups (see above) and it is usually their responsibility to generate ideas for change. The brain storming technique can have a useful, but not essential role here. One of the difficulties is to avoid inflexible thinking and a too literal interpretation of the constraints of the situation. It is quite important that members of the development groups are encouraged to create a positive, problem-solving climate. Once new ideas start to flow, the groups should be encouraged to build upon each other's ideas.

When ideas for redesign have been generated it is necessary to evaluate them. The following procedure would be suitable:

(i) delete hygiene factors from the list
(ii) classify the remaining suggestions in terms of the job characteristics that motivate (*see* chapter 3)
(iii) if the remaining suggestions do not have sufficient motivating characteristics repeat the idea-generating process.

The precise role which employees should play in this process is open to discussion. On the one hand, employees can provide detailed information and suggestions which can only be given by those who know the job intimately. On the other hand, over-exposure to the practicalities of the present job can inhibit a radical, flexible approach. Participation by employees gives greater opportunity for 'gold bricking'.

Three months are usually needed to generate, evaluate and refine ideas for job restructuring.

4 Planning and implementing the change

A programme of work should be drawn up once changes have been identified so that the job redesign can proceed smoothly. A typical outline plan, based upon Carby's (1976) approach, is as follows:

Teach-ins (one month): consist of a series of seminars to explain the objectives of the redesign and to give an understanding of job enrichment and methods. These teach-ins play an important part in allaying fears and creating a conducive atmosphere.

Consultation (three months): to discuss the development group's suggestions and perhaps include wider issues such as the workforce's views on pay, working conditions etc. A motivational survey as described in chapter 4 may provide useful information at this point.

Negotiations (three months): include settling negotiable aspects of the development group's ideas, negotiating with the unions and negotiating within the organization to obtain finance and co-operation from other departments.

Implementation (six months): at this stage the development groups are disbanded and reformulated as implementation groups. The implementation groups monitor the changes and, where appropriate, take action. It should be remembered that the implementation stage does not end until the change has been accepted, or using Lewin's terms 'refrozen' into the organization's behaviour. Abandoning implementation too early can lead to the new job design being rejected in a way that is analagous to the recipient's body rejecting an organ transplant due to insufficient thought being devoted to a patient's post-operative care.

Evaluation (two months): should always be a part of the strategy for job redesign. Some formal assessment based on previously established yardsticks of performance should be undertaken once the new method has had a chance to settle down.

5 *Generalizing the change*

Generalization of the change occurs in two ways. First, the specific job design is adopted at other sites until all those jobs in an organization have been enriched. The second type of generalization has wider implications. In the course of enriching a particular job an organization develops skills and a philosophy towards change in general and so, after an initial project, there should be greater impetus towards changing other aspects of the organization.

An evaluation of job design

Job design, like other management activities, needs proper evaluation otherwise exaggerated or conservative claims will result in resources being allocated in an inefficient way. As in many applications of social science, there is a great danger of exaggerating the outcome because the results are often nebulous and difficult to quantify. Often, outside consultants are commissioned to 'help' the process of job design and there may be a tendency for self-interest to lead to an exaggeration of the benefits from their work. The exaggeration may not be verbal, since it can occur at a subconscious level and the change agents will sincerely believe in the efficiency of their methods. There are psychological pressures on management and employees too. They will have invested considerable time and effort in the job redesign and they will want it to be a success. Pressures of this kind can easily lead to a false consensus of success building up. However, a hard headed business person will want a substantiated answer to the question: 'Does job redesign work?'

A decade ago the answer would almost certainly have been 'Yes, job redesign is better than both motherhood and sliced bread'. Paradoxically after a decade of largely positive case study reports, we are now far less sure. The uncertainty has many sources. We are more aware of the inbuilt pressures to evaluate any change in a positive light. Also, there is an awareness that the mechanisms of reporting case studies and research studies can distort the general impression. The distortion most frequently noted is the tendency for people to publish only their successes. By and large, magazines are reluctant to publish accounts of projects which have gone wrong. Positive findings are much more exciting. Selective reporting can thus produce a false consensus of success. This is not a criticism of job design *per se*. It applies to most studies and investigations but it must colour our view of the general findings emerging from reviews of the literature.

More specific causes of uncertainty about the improvements claimed from job redesign are weaknesses in the underlying theories and the quality of many of the research studies.

Job redesign is implicitly founded on the assumption that workers want enriched jobs. Yet there is relatively little evidence that job enrichment is at the front of employees' minds. Of course, if employees are asked if they would like their jobs enriched, they reply 'yes' in the same way that they would reply 'yes' to any socially desirable suggestion. But when employees are asked less leading questions such

115

as 'What are the things about your job you would like to see improved?' very few mention enrichment. Indeed, the bulk of evidence indicates that employees in the UK and the USA are satisfied with their jobs (Central Statistical Office, 1973 and US Department of Health, Education and Welfare, 1973). When asked questions such as 'If you inherited a very large sum of money would you continue working?' over 80 per cent of employees affirmed that they would continue to work (a similar survey in the UK produced comparable answers (see page 1)). This reply is hardly consistent with mass discontent with the motivational aspects of their jobs. Many social scientists, however, *assume* that employees want enriched jobs (it is interesting to speculate on possible reasons for their assumptions. It could indeed be argued that social scientists themselves tend to be motivated by intrinsic aspects of work and they project these motivations on to others).

Much of the impetus behind the job redesign movement arose from three motivational theories which are popularized in management books and courses. These theories are Maslow's hierarchy of needs, Herzberg's two factor theory and Hackman and Oldham's job characteristic model.

Each of these theories has been subject to biting criticism. As indicated in chapter 2, there are two critical aspects of Maslow's theory: there are five categories of need and they are arranged in hierarchical order. Unfortunately, neither of these has received much empirical support (*see* chapter 2). Herzberg's research has also been criticized (*see* chapter 3). Perhaps the most vociferous criticism concerns Herzberg's interpretation of his results. In essence, it is argued that the results reflect attribution theory rather than motivation of employees. We tend to attribute nice things (motivators such as achievement, responsibility etc) to ourselves while we tend to attribute nasty things (the physical conditions, supervisors etc) to our environment. Even Hackman and Oldham's job attribute approach has not withstood critical investigation entirely (*see* chapter 3). The criticisms of the theories underlying job design are sufficient to arouse doubts about job enrichment. These doubts are supplemented by doubts over the quality of the scientific procedures adopted in many of the studies which showed improvements due to job enrichment. Often the weakness consists of ignoring the Hawthorne effect. In addition many studies have contaminated their results with other causes and wrongly attributed the improvement to job enrichment.

Almost everyone is familiar with the Hawthorne effect. It is one of the oldest and best established findings in industrial psychology. It states that almost any change, even trivial changes in the working environment or job will bring about an improvement in productivity because, presumably, employees respond to the interest that is being taken in them. The Hawthorne effect adds many complications to the scientific evaluation of changes in working methods. If studies are to carry any scientific weight, they must involve two groups, an experimental group and a control group: the experimental group undergoes a real change such as job enrichment while the control group undergoes a trivial change such as having the walls repainted. The change in working method is only significant if the improvement by the experimental group is greater than the improvement by the control group. Unfortunately, many of the job enrichment studies have not adopted this design. They consist of simple case studies or a before and after design. Consequently, many of the improvements claimed for job design could instead be attributed to the well known Hawthorne Effects.

The second criticism levelled at job design studies is that they have not been controlled for other motivational influences. These other influences have contaminated the results and made them worthless. The Texas Instruments study reported by Weed (1971) is a typical example. Early reports of the study usually made the following points.

Prior to 1967, Texas Instruments' cleaning and janitorial services (at its Dallas, Texas, plant) were carried out by an outside contractor. The company evaluated the plant as only 65 per cent clean. The contractor's ability to do the job well was cramped by a quarterly turnover rate of 100 per cent. Instead of using the contractor's services, the company established its own cleaning teams and designed their jobs with the following criteria in mind:

1 Teams were encouraged to identify problems and to solve them creatively.
2 They were assigned overall job responsibilities with the method of meeting these responsibilities left to them.

3 They developed their own work schedules and operating procedures as teams.

4 They contributed to goal setting for their own jobs.

5 Individuals were assigned specific areas of cleaning responsibility.

Results were:

1 The cleanliness rating improved from 65 per cent to 85 per cent.

2 Number of personnel required for cleaning dropped from 120 to 71.

3 Quarterly turnover dropped from 100 per cent to 9.8 per cent.

However, Fein (1979) in a re-evaluation of job enrichment writes:

> What was not reported by the study was that the outside contractor's employees received only $1.40 per hour. When TI took over the program the starting pay was raised to $1.94 per hour for the first shift, with $1.10 extra added for the second shift and $.20 added for the third. The janitorial employees were given good insurance programs, profit sharing, paid vacations, sick leave, a good cafeteria and working conditions similar to those of other employees at Texas Instruments . . . . (the report) does not mention that in raising the pay by 46 per cent and adding benefits worth one third of their pay, TI was able to recruit better qualified employees.

Clearly the recruitment of better quality employees is equally likely to have caused the improvements noted.

This example is not an isolated one. Fein was able to identify deficiencies in many of the major studies of job enrichment, such as those at General Foods-Topeka, Proctor and Gamble, Polaroid Corporation and AT&T.

Perhaps the most systematic appraisal of job design has been attempted by Locke *et al* (1979). They combed the scientific journals for articles evaluating different methods of motivating workers. They examined each article for its scientific merit and discarded any such as the TI study where the causes could be confounded or confused. Unfortunately, three of the 13 job enrichment studies were borderline cases

Figure 19
Comparison of four motivational techniques

Technique	Number of studies	% median improvement	% showing some improvement	% Range
Money	10	30	100	3 to 49
Goal setting	17	16	100	2 to 58
Job enrichment	10	9	90	−1 to 61
Job enrichment (including questionable studies)	13	17	92	−1 to 63
Participation	16	1	50	−24 to 47

which did not quite live up to the criteria but which still had merit. Using the studies which survived this sifting process, Locke and his colleagues were able to compare the various motivational techniques and the results are summarized in figure 19.

The results are something of a disappointment to the job enrichment movement. Using a number of indicators, job enrichment was less successful in motivating workers than either money incentives or goal setting.

The motivational impact of goal setting and 'high valence' outcomes or reinforcers such as money are discussed in chapter 2. Despite the data in figure 14 it is also worth remembering that performance improvement is not the only aim of most job redesign and enrichment exercises. Improving the quality of working life (QWL) is also a possible target. Improvements in QWL may be worthwhile in their own right, regardless of the changes in productivity.

The next chapter examines a number of job redesign experiments which were specifically designed to bring about improvements in the QWL.

6 Job and work design: some examples

Member countries of the European Economic Community have acknowledged, with Resolution 565, the important and in some cases negative role that work has for many people: '. . . some working conditions have an adverse effect on health and attitudes, therefore, there is a belief that some work should be dramatically changed to take into account worker attitudes'.

The Resolution further recommends the following objectives:

(a) the removal of soul-destroying jobs, as social progress depends on the interest workers take in jobs;
(b) that government authorities, together with employees and work organizations, promote the humanization of working conditions;
(c) more opportunities should be given to workers to participate in the design of methods and conditions of work;
(d) assembly work should be eliminated and consideration given to job enlargement, job enrichment and autonomous work groups;
(e) pay structure should be re-examined in the light of these proposals (Butteriss, 1975).

In EEC member countries and other countries throughout the world such as the USA (see O'Toole, 1973), Japan (Takezawa, 1982) and Sweden (Avergold, 1975) numerous initiatives and experiments designed to improve the Quality of Work Life (QWL), by redesigning and enriching jobs have been carried out. In the UK the Tripartite (the Government, Confederation of British Industry and Trades Union Congress) Steering

121

Group on Job Satisfaction was set up in 1973; the Department of Employment established a Work Research Unit in 1974 with the objective of increasing '. . . The number of organizations that are successfully implementing changes to improve the quality of work life of the people employed in them . . .' (Work Research Unit, 1983).

In very general terms job design can be expected to have a more direct effect on satisfaction and QWL than on performance. The results of Locke *et al*'s (1979) review of the available research presented in chapter 5 (page 118) suggests that job enrichment is not as effective as other approaches in producing improvements in productivity; however redesigning jobs can bring about improvements in factors such as job satisfaction, personal relationships at work, turnover and absenteeism, and employee health as well as performance improvements. For many people outcomes such as these are ends in themselves regardless of productivity improvements.

Goal setting and job design

As chapter 2 makes clear, goals can also play an important role in determining motivation and performance and in terms of job design, goals, as well as the job characteristics discussed in chapter 2, need to be emphasized if productivity is desired.

This emphasis on goals will normally be expressed in terms of clear organizational expectations of required performance standards and feedback on performance levels. In this way, the organization structures both clarity and difficulty levels of employee goals.

Given discretion over goals, the employee will normally emphasize the quality rather than the quantity of performance, presumably because quality is the feature which most clearly defines a 'good worker'. Additional induced pressures are often necessary to ensure that quantity goals are achieved. Collaborative target-setting between superior and subordinate is a good example of induced pressure.

Robert Ford's (1969) account of the enlargement of computer clerks' jobs in the American Telegraph and Telephone Company well illustrates how 'own' and 'induced' pressures operate as motivators. Along with a number of changes intended to increase the clerks' levels of autonomy the following performance criteria were emphasized:

1 Each clerk was given definite assignments and completion dates. With these in mind, clerks scheduled their own work to meet job requirements.

2 Each clerk helped set deadline dates. (Presumably this was done with a superior in 'participative goal-setting' sessions.)

3 Each clerk was given direct feedback on output errors and was to make necessary corrections. Previously this had been done by an assignment clerk or verifier.

Not surprisingly, quality and quantity performance gains were observed. Ford reports similar results for other enlarged clerical jobs.

Forms of job and work design

Job design experiments designed to improve QWL and/or productivity have been conducted for many jobs in a variety of organizations and countries. Taylor's (1975) survey of the 100 best documented international cases of work restructuring found that most were in assembly operations (33 per cent). Semi-skilled machine minding (23 per cent) and process operating (21 per cent) were the next largest groups whilst only 9 per cent were among white collar workers. In the UK a report by the Work Research Unit traced 111 examples of work restructuring schemes. The industries in which these programmes most frequently occurred were chemical, food and drink, engineering, electrical, paper and printing and electronics. Although, consistent with Taylor's findings, few British experiments involve white collar workers, there are exceptions. In 1967, for example, ICI introduced greater autonomy and responsibility for their sales representatives. A subsequent survey showed increased job satisfaction and an 18.6 per cent increase in sales, compared with a control group fall in sales of 5 per cent (Paul and Robertson, 1970).

The impact of new technology

The impact of technological changes on the satisfaction and productivity of miners in British coalfields was reported in the early 1950s by researchers adopting a socio-technical systems approach (Trist and Bamforth, 1951; see chapter 1). Technological change has long been associated with job restructuring and several more recent studies of the links between technological change, job design and worker reactions have been conducted, eg Work Research Unit, 1982. Several studies, rather than attempting to redesign jobs to improve satisfaction or motivation, have concentrated on the impact that technological changes have had on workers. An illustrative study in the UK is that of Buchanan and Boddy (1982). Buchanan and Boddy examined the impact of the introduction of word-processing technology on the characteristics of typing jobs in an engineering consultancy firm employing 500 people in Glasgow.

The introduction of the new technology was linked to changes in output (eg typists produced more using the new technology) but the overall effect on productivity was difficult to assess, since the time that authors waited for reports had not been reduced and authors claimed that they spent more time correcting drafts. The major focus of the study was to assess the impact that the technological change had on job characteristics. Buchanan and Boddy summarize their findings as follows:

> The typist's job in this case was affected in various ways by the introduction of word processing. The change from copy to video typing had reduced task variety, meaning and contribution to end-product, control over work scheduling and boundary tasks, feedback of results, involvement in preparation and auxiliary tasks, skill and knowledge requirements (in some respects) and communication between authors and typists. The change had increased control over typing quality, skill and knowledge requirements (in some respects), and pay and promotion prospects. (p 9)

Buchanan and Boddy go on to argue that the undesirable changes in the typists' jobs were not a necessary outcome of introducing new technology. They argue that management in the organization took decisions to redesign the work that actually reduced variety, meaning and contribution to the end product. There were other options open to management that could have had a more positive effect.

Similar findings concerning lowered satisfaction have emerged from other studies (eg Smith and Quinlan, 1982) although there is also evidence that new technology can be more positively received (Davis and Taylor, 1975; Davis, 1977; Blandy, 1982). Blandy (1982) reports the impact of technological change when the Suffolk Area Ambulance Service introduced a computer, beginning in 1977, to help with planning and vehicle control systems. By 1981 the computer system was functioning well and by early 1982 a more sophisticated computer was introduced. The effects of the new technology included:

the near elimination of tedious, repetitive work. Any that remained was shared amongst the work group
the possibility, welcomed by staff, of learning new skills increased variety
more time available to build up good personal relationships between staff.

What seems clear from the available case studies is that managerial decisions and style can determine whether or not new technology is introduced successfully. To maximize satisfaction, motivation and performance, managers need to consider the basic principles of job design, especially the job characteristics that motivate, and not take decisions and restructure jobs in ways that actually run counter to the principles of job and task design. Smith (1981) has produced *10 dozen basic questions* to help managers, trades unionists and employees who are involved in the introduction of new technology into offices. His questions concerning job design and job considerations are given below:

Job design
Can new jobs be designed so that the tasks combine together to make up satisfying total jobs?
Is each job such that tasks are not too tiring or repetitive?
Is feedback provided on performance levels?
Do jobs contain sufficient variety?
Do jobs contain an element of challenge?
Does the job-holder have responsibility for his/her own work?
Does the job ensure that the skills of the job-holder are well used?

Job considerations
What jobs will be affected?

Are jobs likely to disappear?
What jobs will disappear?
What new jobs will be created?
What functions will be merged?
How many, and which jobs will be changed?
Do we want to avoid de-skilling?
How can we avoid de-skilling?
Can new or remaining jobs be enriched or enlarged?
Are there problems of boredom?
Do the jobs create any kind of stress?
What are the frustrations?
How can the adverse factors be eliminated?

White (1983) has examined the impact of technological change in a variety of settings (eg a sales office, a manufacturing company, a data processing company) and draws attention to the specific problems that supervisors face when new technology is introduced. He suggests that in general supervisors' new jobs make greater calls on interpersonal skills. More specifically, they also have to:

provide more technical leadership
exercise less discipline
deal with fewer individuals
pay greater attention to long term factors
respond to subordinates more frequently
be more concerned with the development of team work
be responsible for more expensive equipment
be more concerned with planning.

Apart from some notable exceptions (eg Volvo's Kalmar plant; Gyllenhammer, 1979) few studies have actually involved changing technology as part of systematic attempts to enrich or enlarge jobs. Furthermore, in cases where changes have not been beneficial, as in some of the studies noted above, the problem has its roots in inappropriate managerial actions rather than technological factors *per se* (*see also* Buchanan and Boddy, 1983). Wall *et al* (1984) discuss this fact and suggest that technological factors and managerial control procedures have their most direct impact on different aspects of job design:

where the design of jobs is concerned with such aspects as

cycle-time, task identity and the nature of cognitive and manipulative skills one can accept the possibility of high degrees of technological determinism. Here change in job characteristics may well require changes to technology. Where, however, one's interest in job design is with the autonomy or control over the planning, execution and task allocation of work, then technology is of less direct relevance. It is managerial philosophy, practice, procedures and structure which are of salience – it is a question of social choice. (p 8).

Work groups

The introduction of semi-autonomous work groups (*see* chapter 3) is probably the single most common tactic in attempts to design jobs that are satisfying and motivating. Autonomous work groups have been introduced into many industries in many countries. Perhaps the most widely known example comes from Volvo's plant at Kalmar, Sweden.

The Kalmar plant was a new factory employing up to 600 people in the south of Sweden and the Volvo management took a deliberate decision to attempt to design jobs that were better from the workers' viewpoint, as well as being efficient. The production processes at Kalmar were based on groups of workers with the following characteristics:

quiet surroundings

individual meeting and rest areas

group responsibility for identifiable portions of the car (eg electrical systems, interiors, doors)

manual controls to override the computer controlling the production flow

group control over the work pace (with the aid of buffer stores for incoming and outgoing cars)

groups responsible for their own inspection

feedback on persistent or recurring problems.

Pehr Gyllenhammer the president of Volvo commented that:

When we started at Kalmar, we made the assumption that the productivity could equal that of any comparable

127

traditional plant. Today we have not one but five new plants, organized in a non-traditional way, all scaled for 600 employees or less. These new plants cost a little bit more to build than traditional factories of similar size, but they are already showing good productivity. We believe productivity will continue to increase because the people who work in them have better jobs. (p 432).

As well as introducing job design principles into small factories Volvo also made significant job design experiments in their larger factories (eg their 8,000 employee plant at Torslanda). The experiments at Torslanda began with job rotation in 1964 and although progress was slow to begin with by 1977 over 60 per cent of relevant employees were involved, as figure 20 reveals. Initial changes in job rotation often paved the way for the formation of rotating employees into self-managing groups.

Figure 20
Changes in percentages of employees involved in job
rotation at Volvo's Torslanda plant

Percentage of (3,000)	1970	1971	1972	1973	1977
assembly people					
involved	3	10	18	30	60+

In his enthusiastic description of Volvo's experiences, Gyllenhammer provides examples from Volvo plants outside Sweden to demonstrate that the same principles seemed to produce positive results in other countries.

Wall and Clegg (1981) describe a case study involving the introduction of semi-autonomous working groups into a medium sized partly-unionized sweet manufacturing company in the UK.

The changes introduced had 3 main elements. First, some modifications in the sweet manufacturing process were designed to enable the introduction of two permanent, leaderless teams who saw the production process through from raw materials to finished sweets; second, changes in the structure of management and supervision brought about a movement of responsibilities away from supervisors to members of the work teams. Specifically, each team was given control over setting the pace of production, the distribution of

128

tasks among team members, the organization of breaks and changeover between different lines, and the allocation of overtime. The role of the supervisor changed accordingly, and the supervisor had the authority to intervene in the team decision-making process *only* if production targets were not being met. In practice, due to various internal staff transfers and changes in responsibility the original structure of one manager, two supervisors and one chargehand was modified to that of one manager (an ex-supervisor) and a clerical assistant. The extent to which all of the personnel changes that took place were planned or coincidental is not clear. The third element of the new design involved the provision of group feedback. The intention here was that the manager would develop a system for providing easy to understand, appropriate and accurate feedback to the work group. As Wall and Clegg put it:

> In short, immediate control over production was transferred to the work groups, whilst management concentrated on providing a support service which maximised the groups' opportunities to work effectively. (pp 411–42).

Before the changes were made the researchers collected data in various forms to provide a picture of the pre-change situation. A questionnaire using a version of the Job Diagnostic Survey (*see* chapters 3 and 4) modified to give group rather than individual results, was one of the measures used. These data revealed lower levels of internal work motivation and general job satisfaction than among comparable groups elsewhere: group autonomy and group feedback scores were also low; mental health scores were less satisfactory than the general population; group work identity scores from the questionnaire were not particularly low, but interviews conducted by the researchers suggested that this feature of work was also important. Work significance and skill variety did not show up as being particularly deficient in the pre-change diagnosis.

The aim of the work redesign experiment was substantially to increase identity, autonomy and feedback. It was hoped that, in turn, changes in these job characteristics would bring about improvements in various outcome variables (ie work motivation, performance, job satisfaction, mental health and labour turnover). Relevant results are shown in figure 21. The results revealed statistically significant changes in the expected direction on all of the relevant outcome variables and on the job characteristics of identity and autonomy, but not feedback.

Figure 21
Results from a group work redesign study
(from Wall and Clegg, 1981)

	Pre-change	Short-term (6 months after changes were made)	Longer-term (18 months after changes were made)
	MEAN SCORES	MEAN SCORES	MEAN SCORES
Internal work motivation	4.78	5.18	5.28
General job satisfaction	4.34	4.68	4.99
Mental health	3.09	1.67	0.50
Performance	11.76	13.93	14.30
Identity	4.68	5.78	5.85
Autonomy	3.29	4.35	4.38
Feedback	2.54	2.42	3.12

An important point to note from this study is that the changes were designed to influence specific job characteristics: identity, autonomy and feedback. Significant changes occurred on two of these characteristics. No attempt was made to influence either variety or significance and no changes occurred in these characteristics. As Wall and Clegg note:

> Lack of differences across time on the measures of perceived skill variety and group work significance are compatible with the exclusion of these variables from the change programme. This supports the validity of the other changes actually recorded which might otherwise be interpreted as the outcome of some generalized form of 'experimenter effect'. (p 42).

Unlike some job redesign case studies this research was well designed, and the authors are careful to consider the possibility that factors other than changes in the internal job characteristics could have brought about the improvements. For example, they consider the possibility that pay changes might have had an impact. In fact less than half of the people in the department received extra pay as a result of the change; these increases averaged less than 10 per cent. They also consider the possibility that improvements in goal-setting may have contributed to the changes. As chapter 2 in this book outlines, goal-setting can have a significant impact on motivation and performance. The authors conclude however that these two factors may well have contributed but 'they seem unlikely to be sufficient in themselves to account for the effects observed.'

Various other aspects of the design make it possible to draw the conclusions that changes in group work design do produce changes in motivation, performance and satisfaction that are consistent with current theories of work design. There is nevertheless a need for more studies that allow clear inferences to be made about the causal factors involved in job redesign using semi-autonomous work groups and outcome variables such as motivation, satisfaction, performance and employee psychological well-being.

Established and greenfield sites

One of the features of any job design case study is whether or not the redesigned jobs are to be conducted at a new, purpose-built (greenfield) site or whether existing facilities are to be used. Volvo's Kalmar plant represents a greenfield site example. However, the majority of published studies refer to situations where jobs have been modified in existing situations.

Some authors (eg Emery, 1980) argue that greenfield sites provide a better basis for designing work. As Kemp *et al* (1983) point out, studies that do focus on greenfield sites are essentially descriptive and do not provide the kind of systematic data that can be used as a basis for making firm scientific inferences. Kemp *et al* (1983) describe a study of their own which investigated the introduction of autonomous work groups in a greenfield site. The study was designed to investigate the following hypotheses:

(i) employees in autonomous work groups perceive higher levels of work complexity (variety, task identity, feedback and autonomy) than their counterparts in conventionally designed jobs; (ii) employees in autonomous work groups

131

perceive associated first-level management behaviour as more considerate and tolerant of individual freedom and less high on initiating structure; and (iii) employees in autonomous work groups report higher levels of work satisfaction, motivation, trust, organizational commitment and mental health. (p 273–4).

The researchers studied four groups of employees, involving one experimental group (day shift, new work design at the new site) and three control groups working under conventional design (evening shift at new site, day and evening shifts at the existing site). Measures of the variables of interest produced mixed support for the hypotheses. Employee perceptions of work complexity, involvement in decision-making, consideration, tolerance of freedom and job satisfaction all produced results that were consistent with the hypotheses. Results concerning motivation, organizational commitment and trust in management were more ambiguous. Scores for the experimental groups were higher, on these variables, than scores for the equivalent shift at the existing site but were not significantly different from scores obtained from workers on the evening shifts at the new or old site. From the point of view of current job design theory the lack of differences on motivation scores is particularly troublesome.

Despite some findings that run counter to theoretical ideas the results of this study are consistent with the idea that there are causal links between job characteristics and job satisfaction in situations where greenfield sites are involved.

Orpen (1979) provides an example of a well-designed study to examine the impact of job changes at an established site.

The research was conducted in the head office of a large quasi-federal agency in the USA. The study involved two groups: a control group (unenriched jobs) and an experimental group (enriched jobs). An important feature of the study is that employees were assigned to either the control or experimental group on a random basis. The exceptions were 'a few' employees who were unwilling to let the company decide which group they should be assigned to. The results for these people were excluded from analysis. This random assignment to groups avoids some of the problems of possible bias when volunteer groups are used for job redesign experiments (Fein,

1979). Pre-change, post-change measures were taken using the Job Diagnostic Survey (JDS) to measure job characteristics: skill variety, task identity, task significance, autonomy and feedback. The JDS and other instruments were used to measure personal outcomes: job satisfaction, job involvement, internal motivation and work outcomes: performance/productivity, absenteeism and turnover. The changes in jobs for the experimental group were designed specifically to 'increase' each of the job characteristics mentioned above. The major elements of the enriched jobs are outlined below:

Employees were not assigned to specific tasks but could decide for themselves which operation to perform and use whichever strategy they preferred to perform a task or set of tasks (designed to improve skill variety).

Employees formed themselves into work units of about 10 people. Each group performed all of the operations necessary on customer requests to form an identifiable unit of work. Previously individual people had done only parts of the whole set of operations (task identity).

Employees received a briefing about the importance of their jobs and how they fitted in to the whole organization (task significance).

Employees were allowed to choose the length and timings of their own breaks and perform their own quality control inspections (autonomy).

The teams of employees posted information about their productivity (number of customer records dealt with) on score boards at the end of each day (feedback).

The results which were collected after six months, in general offer considerable support for job design theory. Each of the three personal outcomes (job satisfaction, job involvement and motivation) were markedly improved and were significantly higher for the experimental group, compared with the control group. Two of the three work outcomes (absenteeism and turnover) were significantly lower for the experimental group. Productivity differences were not observed. Orpen offers several possible reasons for this, including:

confusion amongst members about who should perform tasks

133

an uneconomical trying-out of different working strategies

attempts by employees deliberately to tackle unfamiliar assignments

an inefficient feedback system (many groups did not post their productivity data)

collusion rather than 'healthy competition' between the work units, concerning productivity levels.

These explanations provide several clues as to how such an experiment could be redesigned to maintain the very positive personal and work outcomes achieved *and* produce productivity improvements. Hackman's (1980) comments (*see* chapter 3) on the need for more attention to the design and management of semi-autonomous working groups also appear relevant. Finally, it is interesting and informative to compare this study with a study reported by Locke, Sirota and Woolfson (1976) where changes in absenteeism, turnover *and* productivity were observed after job redesign but attitudinal changes such as job satisfaction *did not* take place.

An overview

Job design case studies have been carried out in many of the developed countries. Examples from the UK, Denmark, the Netherlands, France, West Germany, Italy, Sweden, the USA and Japan are described by Cooper (1977). In general, as noted earlier in this chapter, there are more examples for blue-collar than white-collar workers, and they vary considerably in the types of organization and production systems that are involved.

It is also clear that some aspects of job design theory do not match very well with the data from case studies and several authors have expressed criticisms or reservations about work in this area. Fein (1979) for example has exposed flaws in several studies that were previously thought to provide good evidence on the benefits of job design (*see* page 119) and Blackler and Brown (1978) discuss a number of criticisms. They refer to a review by Srivasta *et al* (1975) which contains over 2,000 references and examines 600 empirical field studies. They state:

Much of the literature is written with a missionary zeal

which leaves the reader in no doubt about the bias of the writer. Bias could affect the validity of the findings in a number of ways: selection of research sites where success is particularly likely, biased perception of consequences, selective reporting of results and the willingness of the subjects to please the researcher. We also have no information concerning the fate of negative results.

A considerable proportion of the studies were subject to threats from instability, mortality, instrumentation, testing and selection interaction. The presence of these threats must weaken our confidence in the findings (quoted in Blackler and Brown pp 37–38).

Some of the major criticisms raised by Blackler and Brown and other authors, eg Hackman, 1977, Kemp *et al*, 1983, are summarized below:

Selective reporting of positive results

Lack of rigorous research designs allowing for clear causal inferences to be drawn

Job design represents a management 'trick' to encourage people to remain satisfied with current management controls and organization practices

When evaluation is conducted, managerially orientated criteria related to the organization's efficiency are used in preference to psychological criteria concerned with personal growth, psychological well-being, and satisfaction, though few studies give clear evaluations of economic benefits

Too little allowance is made in the theory and practice of job design for individual differences between people. For example, White (1977) when discussing work systems using semi-autonomous groups notes that it is not uncommon for work groups to exert pressures on or to exclude altogether individuals regarded as deviant . . . there should be alternative work systems in the same setting, which would cater for those who prefer to work in a particular way. (p 3).

The critical comments warrant attention; nevertheless it is clear that experiments in job design are taking place in a wide set of countries and industries. As the material presented in this chapter indicates, at least some of the theoretical ideas concerning links between job characteristics and outcomes such as work motivation, performance and satisfaction are consistent with the findings of practical experiments. Taken as a whole, the evidence suggests that progress is being made towards designing jobs that are motivating, satisfying and lead to good performance.

7 Motivation at work

The purposes of this chapter are twofold: the first is to provide an outline of Total Quality Management theory integrated with the main practical implications of motivation, and the second is to provide a non-technical résumé of the chapters in the book which can be used by specialists as a briefing on the subject of motivation.

The importance of motivation

Motivation plays an important part both in an individual's and in a company's performance. Even a very well trained and very able employee will not perform well unless motivated. The relationship with performance can be represented by the expression:

$$\text{Performance} = \text{Ability} \times \text{Motivation} \times \text{Training}$$

The expression is not mathematically correct but it demonstrates two major points. First, if motivation is zero, performance will be zero. Secondly, motivation on its own is not enough; it must be accompanied by ability and training. The first point emphasizes the importance of motivation, but the second point emphasizes that, on its own, motivation is not a panacea.

Higher motivation does not always result in a direct increase in productivity, because, in many jobs, productivity is limited by other people or by the pace of machines. For example, higher motivation among production-line workers will not result in higher productivity because the speed of the line will determine the pace of the work, and the speed of the line will often be adjusted to the speed of one of the slower workers. Similarly, increased motivation may not result in increased sales by a newspaper vendor, for example, since the occurrence of newsworthy events and the number of readers who pass the news stand are more direct influences on sales. However, the absence of a direct link between productivity and motivation does not mean that managers can afford to ignore the subject. There are situations where the motivation of individuals has a direct effect. Furthermore, motivation is important even in those jobs paced by external events.

Psychologists have established quite strong relationships between job satisfaction and lateness, absenteeism and quitting a job. It would seem that if jobs do not satisfy people's motives employees will tend to withdraw from the job whenever the slightest excuse arises. In most organizations, the consequences of such withdrawal of work, in the form of lateness, absenteeism and labour turnover, have a direct impact on profitability.

Individual differences in motivation

A moment's reflection about the motivation of members of a work group will confirm that not everyone has the same level of motivation. The exact reason why is not clear but there are two main possibilities: some people may innately have a higher level of motivation than others; some may be influenced by their experience of life to be more motivated than others. The innate aspect of motivation exists but it accounts best for biological needs such as hunger, sleep and warmth, which are not directly relevant to the motivation of employees in industry. A person's general level of work-related motivation is important, however, and it can be useful to select people whose level of motivation is generally high. Heredity may play a part in determining which direction this high level of motivation will take but the direction of motivation is often best explained in terms of learning and past experience.

The differences among people in the level and direction of their motivation do not occur at random. To an extent they reflect other characteristics such as a person's age, sex and occupation. Each of these can be considered in greater detail.

Age and motivation

Undoubtedly motivation changes with age but it is difficult to specify the exact nature of the changes. Research findings often arise as a by-product of work in other areas and the results are scattered over a variety of publications. For example, Wolk and Kurtz (1975) found that older people had a more internal frame of reference and reported their surprising result in the *Journal of Consulting and Clinical Psychology*. Under most assumptions, older people could be expected to be more externally oriented, ie to believe that things happen to them because of events over which they have no control. However, Wolk and Kurtz suggest that their findings arose because the older groups in their investigation were brought up in a more 'internal' era when people were encouraged to believe that they were the arbiters of their own fate.

Results concerning job satisfaction are available from a survey of 1,302 people in Manchester. The survey was conducted by the students of Manchester School of Management (UMIST) and the findings are given in figure 22. Mancunians of all ages are most satisfied with their colleagues and the supervision they receive. Mancunians of all ages are least satisfied with their pay and prospects of promotion. Within this framework of agreement across the age spectrum some interesting age differences emerge. Satisfaction with work tends to increase with age but there is a dip in satisfaction in

Figure 22
Satisfaction scores for different age groups

the 40–50 years age group which suggests that it is probably the least satisfied and is the group that is most difficult to motivate. In particular, satisfaction with promotion prospects falls to very low levels at age 40–50 before rising again. This may help to explain the successful initiative developed by the DIY store B&Q, which began a recruitment campaign in the late 1980's to attract over-50's. One store (Macclesfield) was staffed entirely by over-50's (except for the manager) and produced far better than average sales and customer satisfaction. The age distribution within an organization forms an implicit career timetable, and people use this timetable to decide whether their own career is on or off schedule. In one study, managers who saw themselves as 'behind time' had more negative attitudes to work than other managers.

Sex and motivation

Figure 23 depicts satisfaction levels for five areas and it allows the levels of men and women to be contrasted. Men's satisfaction is shown by the height of the blocks nearer the reader and women's satisfaction is shown by the height of the blocks further from the reader. It can be seen that the pattern of satisfaction is very similar for the sexes: they tend to be most satisfied with supervision and colleagues and least satisfied with pay and promotion. However, there are some differences of emphasis. Women tend to be more satisfied than men with their colleagues and, to a slight extent, their supervisors. They are less satisfied than men with their promotion prospects, and the type of work they do, and they are much less satisfied than men with their pay.

Occupational groups and motivation

Most people would expect substantial differences in the satisfaction of the various occupational groups. The survey of Mancunians certainly supports this view and it indicates that some of the largest differences exist between those who work full-time and those who work part-time. Part-time workers were noticeably less satisfied with their pay, promotion prospects and the type of work they do. However, part-time workers were rather more satisfied with the company of their colleagues. Figure 24 portrays the differences in satisfaction

140

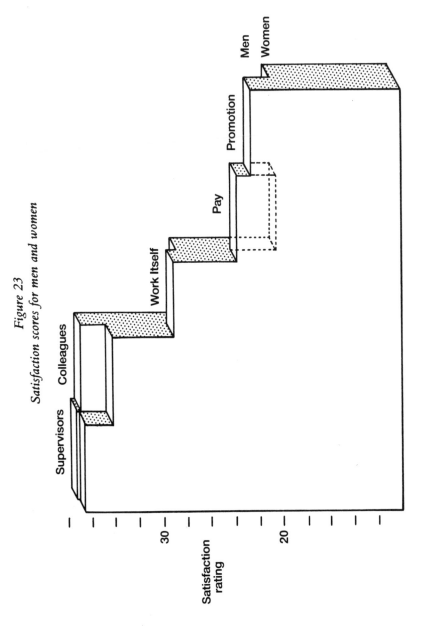

Figure 23
Satisfaction scores for men and women

141

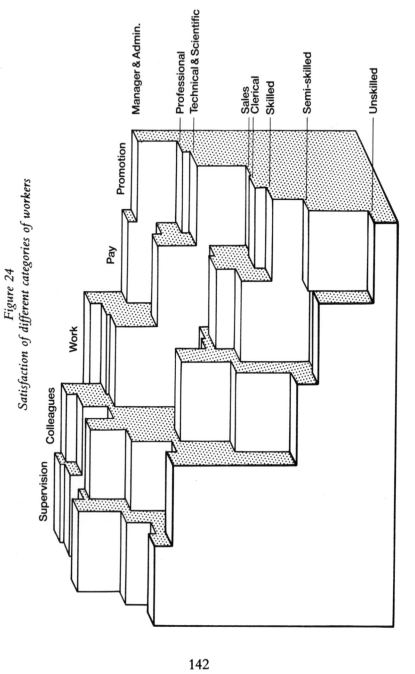

Figure 24
Satisfaction of different categories of workers

between different categories of workers and shows satisfaction levels. Figure 24 opposite shows satisfaction levels in the same five areas as the previous figure. Satisfaction for different occupational groups is shown by the height of the blocks. The blocks nearest the reader show the satisfaction for unskilled workers while the blocks furthest from the reader show managers' satisfaction, etc. Again, there is the tendency in all groups for supervision and colleagues to be the most satisfying areas of work whereas pay and promotion are seen to be the least satisfying. There is also a strong tendency for managers, professional and technical staff to be more satisfied in all areas than blue-collar workers. The main exceptions to these general trends were an unexpectedly high level of satisfaction among skilled operatives concerning the type of work they perform, and clerical staff were happier than might be expected with the company of their colleagues.

Managers are the occupational group whose motives have been studied in greatest depth. Porter *et al.* (1975) used Maslow's much criticized (*see* chapter 2) model of motivation to investigate the needs of different levels of managers. As Maslow's theory would predict, senior managers have unmet needs concerning self-realization, middle managers have need deficits relating to autonomy and self-realization, while junior managers have large need deficits in all aspects except security and social fulfilment. In a nutshell, Porter *et al*'s research indicates that senior managers have reached the top of Maslow's hierarchy, whereas junior managers are still at the middle levels.

A great deal of work has been carried out on the achievement motivation (nAch) of managers. Although is is not an identical concept, nAch may, in some ways, be related to the level of growth need strength (GNS) that different individuals display (*see* chapter 3, p 64). A fuller description of this research is given in Smith *et al* (1982). In essence, results from studies in the USA, UK, Mexico, India, Australia and Finland show that companies whose executives have high achievement motivation produce better results. This is particularly true in an entrepreneurial rather than a bureaucratic organization. For example, one study examined the motives of 51 technical entrepreneurs and also calculated the growth rate of their companies in terms of value of sales. The growth rate of those companies led by entrepreneurs with high nAch was almost 250 per cent higher than that of companies led by entrepreneurs with moderate nAch. Another important line of research arose from the work of McClelland: the leadership motive pattern. Achievement motivation is usually measured alongside the motives for power and for affiliation. It was noted that a certain pattern enabled people to be effective managers at the higher levels in an organization. It was found that, with senior managers, success tends to be associated with a low level of affiliation motive and a moderate to high need for power, together with an ability to inhibit spontaneous impulses (McClelland and Boyatzis, 1982), but with lower level managers success was related to a combination of both high need for power and a high need for achievement. These findings were given additional support by Stahl (1983) in a study of 172 managers. Stahl (1983) used a job choice exercise (JCE) measure, in place of the thematic apperception test (TAT) used previously by McLelland and others, which has been demonstrated to be both unreliable and invalid (Fineman, 1977). Stahl found that those who scored high on both need for power and achievement exhibited better managerial performance and also had a correspondingly higher promotion rate than others. The opposite was true for those who scored low on these needs. Other measures that are predictive of effective managerial potential (Mp) include the California Psychological Inventory (CPI). Gough (1984) used this measure on a sample of 143 military officers, and showed that those who scored high on the dimension of Mp tended to be productive, goal-directed, ambitious and socially adept. Conversely, those with lower Mp scores tended to be erratic, self-defeating, given to mood swings and vulnerable to threat. Taken as a whole these findings suggest that a manager's motivating potential appears to be predictive of effective managerial behaviour, which at a practical level has implications for selection procedures.

Managerial action and motivation

Most managers are concerned with increasing the motivation of employees but often wonder what action they can take to achieve their aim. In practice, managers may influence motivation in five main ways: ensuring that the environment is motivating; selecting highly motivated employees; training; appraisal; and remuneration.

Total Quality Management

Currently, in response to increasing competition and European product liability legislation, the improvement of the quality of products and services has become a key element of the commercial policy of organizations. These quality issues are typically being addressed by the advocacy and adoption of the Japanese management technique of Total Quality Management (TQM), which promises to increase long-term business performance and profitability (Peters, 1987). TQM is an organization-wide philosophy that links product and service quality to customer satisfaction by institutionalizing planned and continuous quality improvement, the purpose of which is to provide a common focus for all employees, so that individuals with different tasks, abilities and priorities are able to communicate in pursuit of a common organizational goal (Wilkinson, 1992). The focus is upon providing quality products and services to customers.

A certain amount of confusion exists, however, with the precise definition of quality, which has led to problems in defining the management of quality. Quality has variously been defined as 'conformance to requirements' (Crosby, 1979), 'fitness for use' (Juran, 1979), 'a predictable degree of uniformity and dependability, at low cost and suited to the market' (Deming, 1986), 'a moving target defined by the customer' (Feigenbaum, 1983) and 'zero defects' (Collard, 1989). Essentially, these definitions are variations of the same theme (Oakland, 1989) but with emphases upon 'technical' or 'functional' quality (Groonroos, 1984). To overcome problems in defining the management of quality, Hill (1991) divided the concept of quality into two separate but related aspects. First, quality of design is defined as 'conformance to the requirements of the customer', and emphasizes that to be effective a product or service must meet the needs of the customer and not the convenience of the producer. Second, achieving the required quality design is dependent upon the efficiency of operations performed within a company. The efficiency of operations is involved in Juran's (1988) concept of self-control, whereby responsibility for quality should be assigned only to individuals who in fact control the quality of what they do. Individuals need to have both the ability to regulate what they do and, crucially, the authority to implement improvements, within certain boundaries. The concept of self-regulation of task activities has not only been demonstrated to sustain effort but, more important, has been shown to lead to continuous improvement of task activities through self-development (Bandura, 1988). In turn this may reduce employees' dependence on tasks assigned by superiors. Self-control and self-regulation are related aspects of self-determination, which has been shown to be a key feature of semi-autonomous work groups in the management of their everyday work (Wall and Martin, 1987). Self-determination typically involves collective control over the pace of work, the distribution of tasks within the group, and the timing and organization of breaks. Often these groups require little or no direct supervision (Emery, 1980). Thus the introduction of semi-autonomous work groups (*see* chapter 3) would facilitate the conditions necessary to fulfil Juran's concept of greater self-control among lower-level employees.

A powerful motivator and rationale for the management of quality is the cost of quality failures. Traditionally, quality costs have been narrowly defined as the cost of running a quality department, coupled with scrap and rework charges (Bright, 1991). Increasingly it has been accepted that, in addition to the costs associated with failures of systems and products, quality costs are incurred in the design, implementation, operation and maintenance of quality management systems. The notion that getting quality right causes productivity to fall, with associated increases in costs, is incorrect (Dale and Plunkett, 1990). For example, the cost of rework is usually higher than that of inspection; similarly, the cost of inspection is often higher than that of prevention. Avoidable failure costs have been estimated to be 95 per cent of the total cost of quality, which can be pruned by two-thirds in three years if TQM systems are implemented (Plunkett and Dale, 1990). Oakland (1989) estimates that approximately one-third of all effort expended in British businesses is wasted because of the snowball effect that errors have in creating problems in different departments of an organization. Further, it has been estimated that less than 40 per cent of senior managers are aware of the costs of quality in their organizations (Plunkett and Dale, 1990). When analysed and identified, quality costs can be used to display the importance of quality-related activities to management in meaningful terms, and provide a significant management tool for initiating improvement projects. However, focusing only on quality cost reduction as a device to increase commitment to TQM may be detrimental, in that TQM may be perceived as a cost-cutting exercise or a productivity improvement programme, and as such is likely to be unsuccessful (Oakland, 1989).

It has been estimated that approximately 80 per cent of Total Quality initiatives fail to reach their potential (Atkinson, 1990) in the UK. This may be due to a number of individual or cumulative factors, such as:

1 *Failure to appreciate the time scale involved* (Botterill, 1991). This may lead to the rejection of ideas that do not fulfil their promise (Oakland, 1989). Advocates of the quality movement argue that quality improvement is an on-going process that can take between five and ten years to become embedded in an organization's culture (Lascelles and Dale, 1990). Botterill (1991) found that the completion of initial 'awareness-building' projects usually takes between 12 and 18 months. It is important for organizations to recognize that quality improvement is a long and arduous journey which has no end.

2 *Not recognizing the full implications of TQM* and the impact upon the business as a whole (Dumas, 1989). Typically, this has consisted of focusing upon and allocating up to 80 per cent of resources to 'hard' aspects such as technical training and installing new production systems. This implies that less than 20 per cent of resources have been devoted to 'soft' aspects such as management training in the underlying philosophy of TQM and personnel involvement in quality programmes. Neglecting the 'soft' aspects may lead to a demotivated workforce.

3 *Lack of senior management commitment to the quality process* (Atkinson, 1990). This may derive from the fact that senior managers do not view themselves as part of the quality problem but see it as a worker motivation issue, or do not realize that implementing TQM requires a change in their own attitudes and behaviour (Dumas, 1989). The commitment of senior managers may be important in a variety of

ways. First, they influence organizational values. Second, they influence the quality infrastructure that is concerned equally with the 'hard' and 'soft' aspects of performance. Third, they provide a role model to others, by modelling, or failing to model, the behaviour expected in the new quality management system.

4 *Resistance to change*, which may be overt or covert, at both the individual and the organizational level (Smith *et al*, 1982). Change often involves the unknown and may be perceived as a threat. For example, at the individual level, the traditional policing role of many supervisors or managers is inappropriate for encouraging 'ownership' of quality. The role needs to be replaced with participative strategies. This may be perceived as deskilling, and threatening to their authority, unless training in interpersonal skills and participative decision-making is provided prior to changes taking place. Similarly, change at the organizational level will be resisted if it is perceived as a threat to existing power bases (Hellriegal *et al*, 1989). The resistance may be ameliorated by discussion of the problems and possible courses of action with all those affected, provided there is willingness to adapt plans in the light of the discussions (Child, 1987).

5 *Uncertainty about how to implement a quality improvement programme* (Bright, 1991). There is no single route to success. Different management styles and corporate cultures will need to take different paths. What is essential is that quality programmes must start at board level, with senior management gaining an understanding of the fundamental principles, and deciding how those principles can best be applied in practice (Dale and Plunkett, 1990).

In the long term there is a necessity for the introduction of both quality systems and a quality culture to facilitate the quality process. A quality culture is defined as 'a culture that nurtures high-trust social relationships and respect for individuals, a shared sense of membership of the organization, and a belief that continuous improvement is for the common good' (Hill, 1991). The extent to which the prescriptions of TQM will develop such a culture has yet to be subjected to rigorous scientific scrutiny; and although advocates of TQM can point to various successes, many of the fundamental con-

148

cepts and procedures are best seen as potentially useful rules of thumb rather than as scientifically validated principles.

Introducing quality systems and a quality culture has implications for organizations in terms of changes in spans of control, work and job design, training, motivation strategies, reward systems and appraisal systems.

Designing a motivating environment

Some organizations seem to have been designed in a way that is calculated to reduce the motivation of their employees; the organizational climate is restrictive and it emphasizes a passive role for employees. In other organizations the climate is participative and encouraging. One of the first studies of the influence of organizational climate was by Andrews (1967), who compared two Mexican companies. One of these organizations valued achievement and the president freely shifted people around to make use of their abilities. The second organization had a climate which did not value achievement. It was headed by an unpredictable man who ran his empire like a feudal hacienda and at 'command performance' staff meetings he would give his executives a public dressing down. Not surprisingly Andrews found that promotion in the first organization correlated with an executive's achievement motivation while in the second it was related to his power motive. Interestingly, the first organization succeeded and increased its profitability and markets, while the second stagnated.

Total Quality Management systems assume that quality is the outcome of all the activities that take place within an organization, and therefore all functions and employees must participate in the improvement process. Senior management provide the main impetus, by determining quality priorities, establishing quality management systems and the procedures to be followed, in conjunction with the provision of resources and leading by example. Despite this involvement of top management, quality improvement is intended to flow from proactive participation and co-operation on the part of organizational units and employees. Various assumptions underpin this position. The first is that everyone in an organization has relevant knowledge and experience to contribute to the improvement of efficiency and effectiveness (Hill, 1991).

Research has demonstrated (Wilson, 1991) that participative group processes release analytical and creative talents in participants, so that topics inevitably include job design issues of role content, autonomy, training, communication, interest and job satisfaction. These topics are directly relevant to the principles governing the implementation of TQM. Second, traditional managerial practices and organizational arrangements do not harness this potential to contribute in a satisfactory manner. Any organization which uses the knowledge and insights of its employees in the analysis, specification and implementation of change is utilizing a key company resource more fully. Moreover, not only does the harnessing of this resource aid in the implementation of TQM, it has also been shown to enhance the self-confidence, competence and independence of employees involved (Mambrey *et al*, 1987). These attributes are key causal variables in determining levels of performance (Bandura, 1982), motivation and job satisfaction (Hackman and Oldham, 1976) and are supported by research evidence from investigators who are not directly associated with the quality movement. Third, given the right setting, most people welcome the opportunity to contribute to quality improvement. Ford (1969) showed that, given discretion over goals, employees normally emphasized the quality rather than the quantity of performance. The explanation was that quality was the feature that most clearly defined a 'good worker'.

It is crucial, however, that four underlying principles are adhered to in creating the right setting for participation (French and Caplan, 1973). First, the change process must not be used as a means of manipulation (e.g. employees' advice is sought but subsequently ignored) which can be construed as a sham. Second, the decisions to be made must not be seen as trivial or unimportant, as this is likely to undermine the motivation of participants. Third, those tasks and activities upon which participation is based must be relevant both to the needs of workers and to continuing quality improvement. Fourth, those participating in the decision-making must have the legitimacy and authority to implement any decisions made. Underlying this fourth point is the assumption that individuals are more likely to be committed to quality improvements on a daily basis if they are involved in making the relevant decisions. Participative decision-making encourages individual 'ownership' of the improvement process, which usually manifests itself through increased commitment to the solution's success (Imada and Robertson, 1987), and performance (Kanfer, 1992), which is enhanced further by the openness of the involvement (Hollenbeck *et al*, 1989). Moreover, there is a reduction in undesired side effects and after-effects (Reuter, 1987).

Organization structure

An organization's structure has implications for motivation. Indik (1965), for example, showed the size of an organization as related to symptoms of poor motivation such as absence and turnover. He suggested that large organizations tend to be less motivating because they are more structured and define jobs more rigidly. The work of other researchers suggests that the relationship between size and motivation is complex, and what really matters is not the size of the whole organization but the size of the sub-unit of which the individual is a part.

Total Quality Management is seen as a behaviourial intervention that builds up the awareness, understanding, motivation and commitment of employees at all levels (Collard, 1989). Quality becomes the responsibility of everyone in an organization and is not delegated to a specialist department. It therefore follows that the quality of the final product or service is dependent upon many activities in an organization. It is helpful if these activities can be reviewed and integrated into a holistic process. Oakland (1989) states that 'The key to motivation and quality is for everyone in the organization to have well defined customers'. Thus creating an internal market, whereby each organizational unit is both an internal 'customer' and 'supplier', stresses the importance of understanding and meeting customer needs. These concepts may be relatively easy to introduce into commercially driven environments, but it may prove more challenging to introduce them into some organizations where customers and products do not share the same language. It remains to be seen whether or not quality improvement can have a sustained and beneficial impact on working practices in a wide range of organizational settings.

As a customer the unit expects conformity to its own requirements from other units: as a supplier it is obliged to conform to the requirements of other units. These organizational units, including both line and support functions, become part of a quality chain that emphasizes that all employees are ultimately responsible in serving the final, external customer. This approach is often referred to as 'customer care'. Wilkinson and Witcher (1991) postulate that the internal market should include quality infrastructure and regulations (including internal customer rights). They also indicate some overlap with personnel matters such as recognition, rewards, pay systems, employee support and training, all of which will affect the motivation of employees. The introduction of an internal market can be construed as providing an opportunity to create a climate which emphasizes and rewards appropriate achievement. This suggests that a manager's first step in motivating his workforce is ensuring that the characteristics of a motivating environment (*see* figure 25) are in place within each organizational unit.

Quality improvement and the introduction of quality systems may necessitate changes in the structure of an organization (Hill, 1991). The oversight and direction of the improvement process will normally reside in a steering committee of senior managers, who report direct to the top of the organization. This steering committee allocates responsibility to subsidiary units for the attainment of corporate quality policies, determines the procedures to be employed and monitors outcomes. Subsidiary units set up similar committees that report to their local senior management. Because quality management involves a greater flow of information outside the normal vertical lines of communication, horizontal arrangements are needed for organized communication, between departments and across functions. Cross-functional management is therefore crucial to the success of TQM. Examples of horizontal activity include the principle of internal markets, whereby each organizational unit (eg division, department, section) is both a customer and supplier. While internal marketing should improve coordination and enhance communication, in practice there is a need for formal arrangements, such as the creation of multi-functional and interdepartmental project teams. The conditions for creating highly motivated project teams are discussed in chapter 3. Wherever naturally occurring groups are to be found within the existing structure they should be formalized and given responsibility for identifying and solving quality problems that are within their areas of responsibility and competence. Membership of these groups

152

Figure 25
Characteristics of a motivating environment

1 Employees have a realistic understanding of the links between effort and performance, ie they know how hard they need to work to reach various levels of performance.

2 Employees have the competence and confidence to translate effort into performance.

3 Control systems are introduced only when necessary.

4 Performance requirements are expressed in terms of hard, but attainable, specific goals.

5 Employees participate in setting goals.

6 Feedback to employees is regular, informative and easy to interpret.

7 Employees are praised for good performance.

8 Rewards (including pay) are seen as equitable.

9 Rewards are tailored to individual requirements and preferences.

10 Employee psychological and physical well-being is recognized as important.

11 Productivity is recognized as important.

12 Jobs are designed, where possible, to maximize:

    skill variety
    task identity
    task significance
    autonomy
    feedback
    opportunities for learning and growth.

13 Organization and job changes are brought about through consultation and discussion, not by fiat.

should be flexible and relevant, with no vertical or horizontal constraints (Wilkinson and Witcher, 1991). Wilson and Grey (1986) identified several factors crucial to the introduction of semi-autonomous work groups. The process must be slow and iterative; this may lead to criticisms of increased development time, cost and effort. However, the criticisms could be a blessing in disguise if they lead to a more reflective, universal and broad-based approach in development. The process must be paralleled by a system of training and support. For example, members of the group may need training in participative decision-making. Conventional forms of communication and bargaining, and a certain amount of prescriptive decision-making, may sometimes be required to facilitate the initial open, group-led changes. The introduction of participation in problem-solving and decision-making is likely to have an effect beyond its original focus and boundaries, either through the content or through the process of participation strategies, (Wilson, 1991). Therefore participative methods will not only enhance the motivation of individual employees, they will have an impact upon other organizational units. For example, increasing the autonomy of assembly work groups may have a ripple effect that impacts upon the purchasing or maintenance departments. In the context of TQM, this effect can be beneficial, in that it may allow an evolutionary approach toward redesigning an organization's structure. For example, if autonomous work groups, utilizing participative decision methods, were introduced systematically into key areas of an organization the impact upon other departments could be evaluated. Those departments that were significantly affected would be the next key areas to introduce participation and the principles of TQM. Not only would this evolutionary process allow the identification of naturally occurring work groups, and highlight areas where interdepartmental project teams are essential, it would also provide a systematic basis for reorganizing support functions, communication systems, producing codes of practice for autonomy, redesigning reward systems and redefining work measurement systems. This evolutionary approach to implementing TQM systems is supported by Boaden *et al* (1991), who state that 'Experience suggests that small incremental changes are the best means of facilitating culture change and holding the gains made.'

One type of organizational structure that may facilitate the creation and coordination of committees, project teams and semi-autonomous work groups is that of a matrix design (Hill, 1991). This offers the advantage of explicitly linking the structure with consumer markets (Lawrence and Lorsch, 1967) and technological change (Burns and Stalker, 1961). Moreover, it incorporates the conflicting requirements of both uniformity and diversity pressures (Handy, 1976). A typical matrix design structure retains the normal vertical hierarchy within and between functional departments, but is 'overlaid' with horizontal communication channels (*see* figure 26). This involves a partial abandonment of the principle that organizational authority has to be hierarchically arranged, and replacing it with the notion that communication is enhanced by managers and workers who talk to each other on the basis of who has relevant information, rather than who reports to whom (Galbraith, 1977). Such an organizational form permits higher information processing capacity without duplication of people but, conversely, forces people into new behaviour patterns (Schein, 1980). In practice, this involves assigning specialists from specific functional departments to work with one or more interdisciplinary work teams that are led by project leaders. When the particular project task is complete, team members return to their functional departments or join other interdepartmental teams. Thus the essence of a matrix design is the enhancement of flexibility within a 'multiple command system' (Davis and Lawrence, 1977) in which employees have two or even more bosses to whom they are equally accountable (e.g. their functional department manager and their project manager).

Figure 26
The matrix structure of Marks and Spencer's engineering department
(from Tse, 1985)

The advantages claimed for matrix structures include releasing top management's time from problems of operational coordination; exposing specialists to situations where they need to take account of other disciplinary viewpoints, which should broaden their outlook and enhance their self-development; the delegation of some authority to lower levels of management, which can provide additional motivation, particularly to junior management, who have the opportunity to influence critical decisions; and the encouragement of competition between organizational units, which may provide the impetus to innovation and achievement (Child, 1987).

Possible areas of conflict need to be addressed in order for smooth transitions to take place. For example, changes in an organization's structure will affect the distribution of authority, as well as lateral relationships between work groups within the overall work flow system. If these effects are not recognized, or are resisted, the policy of redesign may well be threatened or stifled. For example, the introduction of semi-autonomous work groups might be viewed by junior and middle management as detrimental to their authority, with subsequent effects upon their motivation. In practice, however, these layers of management are relieved of the everyday pressure of 'fire-fighting', progressing work and materials or reallocating people to machines and tasks, and instead are able to devote more time to coordinating work groups, developing their members' abilities, taking part in recruitment and dealing with important technical problems (Child, 1987), which enhances their status. Middle managers play a crucial pivotal role, as they stand at the crossroads of the vertical and horizontal planes in a matrix design, and are responsible for quality improvement activities undertaken by their subordinates (Ishikawa, 1985). This pivotal role may fulfil middle management's need for autonomy and self-realization (Porter et al, 1975), as they will be in a position to orchestrate strategy development and create a high-trust motivational environment.

Chapter 1 suggested that structure, technology and climate are important factors in maintaining a motivated workforce. Similarly, it was noted that the organization's structure arises from, and also gives rise to, the implicit models which managers have of the way their employees are motivated. However, chapter 1 also made the point that the exact influence of organizational characteristics, such as structure and climate, is difficult to specify. The way these influences work is indirect. The relationships are complex, and it is difficult to establish clear trends. The motivation of individuals is much more directly affected by the models of motivation that managers adopt (*see* chapter 2), the detailed design of jobs (*see* chapter 3) and the selection, training, appraisal and remuneration of employees than by macro-organizational structure.

Control systems

The type of control systems which an organization uses to ensure that employees perform their duties also has a direct influence on the level and direction of an employee's motivation. Chapter 1, for example, quoted a case study (Blau, 1955) from a government employment agency in which the control system deflected the direction of employees' motivation. The staff of the agency were responsible for interviewing clients, helping them to complete application forms, counselling them on suitable jobs and referring them to jobs. As a basis for evaluating its staff the agency kept a record of the number of interviews conducted by each member of staff. Blau writes:

An instrument intended to further the achievement of organizational objectives . . . constrained interviewers to think of maximizing the indices as their major goal, sometimes at the expense of these very objectives. They avoided operations which would take up time without helping them to improve their numbers . . . and wasted their own and the public's time on activities intended only to raise the figures on their record.

Babchuck and Goode (1951) provide a similar example, of a selling unit in a department store, which judged employees' performance in terms of sales volume. Total sales increased but the longer-term goals of the organization were imperilled by 'sales grabbing' and the neglect of unmeasured functions such as stock work and arranging the displays of goods. Therefore the measures used to assess various aspects of performance have to be designed and applied in such a way that detrimental effects upon other areas of performance are minimized.

157

One of the most difficult but important aspects of TQM is measuring quality (Botterill, 1991). Traditionally, product quality has been concerned with physical attributes. Levitt (1980), however, postulates that quality involves a number of further elements, beyond physical attributes, and that a physical product must be thought of as possessing elements previously associated with 'services' only. Lascelles and Dale (1990), following research in British manufacturing industries, found that clearly stated and measurable quality objectives and providing regular feedback to all participants were crucial aspects of success in implementing TQM. Similarly, in a study of air conditioning manufacturers in Japan and the USA, Garvin (1983) found that strong performers in terms of quality management utilized goal-setting and cross-functional participation in conjunction with high managerial support. (*See* chapter 2 for a discussion of goal-setting.)

Performance measurement and feedback systems can be powerful tools in attempts to enhance organizational productivity (Algera, 1990). Feedback is seen as a necessary component of the functioning of a system, preventing entropy and enabling adaptation. Organizations, however, are not automatically self-correcting, and the process of attending to, interpreting and acting on feedback is crucial (Katz and Kahn, 1966). Immediacy of feedback facilitates error correction and problem-solving (Nadler, 1979); in addition, it serves to affect motivation positively, cues individuals as to what an organization considers proper performance, and enables individual learning (Vroom, 1964). Individuals in organizations have been shown to engage actively in feedback-seeking behaviour (Ashford and Cummings, 1983) through 'monitoring' or 'enquiry' strategies, both of which constitute important means of obtaining information (Herold and Parsons, 1985). However, by providing everyone with the necessary tools and systems that provide feedback, the need to seek information is minimized.

The tools and systems used to provide feedback, both to individuals and to other organizational units, will of necessity have to be concerned with both the 'hard' and the 'soft' aspects of performance. Within TQM, 'hard' aspects typically involve a range of production techniques such as statistical process control, 'Just in Time' inventory control, and changes in the layout of work stations, design processes and the procedures of the organization. These production techniques are generally analysed by process flow charting, tally charts, Bareto analysis, scatter diagrams, histograms, control charts and cause-and-effect analysis. The 'soft' aspects of TQM are largely concerned with attitudes, commitment 'and culture change' within an organization (Hendricks and Triplett, 1989). This can be brought about by creating customer awareness, and increasing personnel's motivation and commitment to the quality process. Oakland (1989) states that

> the objective of TQM is to make everyone accountable for their own performance, and to get them committed to attaining quality in a *highly motivated fashion* [author's italics]. The assumptions a director or manager must make in order to move in this direction are simply that people want to achieve, accomplish, influence activity and challenge their abilities.

This view reflects the attributes of Theory Y expressed in McGregor's (1960) concept of Theory X and Theory Y, which distinguishes between two divergent approaches to managing people and tasks. Theory X is based upon the premise that individuals are not self-motivated and must be directed, persuaded, rewarded, or even browbeaten in order to submit to the needs of the organization. This view presupposes that people are lazy, dislike responsibility and are insensitive to organizational goals. Theory Y is based upon the premise that individuals are primarily self-motivated and self-controlled and want to influence decisions, to be morally involved in their work organization, and to be able to use their skills and abilities in the service of the organization. This view is consistent with the values of self-determination and greater participation at work.

Thus the 'soft' aspects also include Human Resource Management, which has typically been ignored by TQM writers, reflecting their production orientation (Wilkinson *et al*, 1991). Seddon (1989) has argued that the failure of many TQM programmes to achieve 'culture change' is due to management paying insufficient attention to the underlying values and behaviour of employees. Because TQM is a holistic process it is necessary to give equal weight to both the 'hard' and the 'soft' aspects of an organization. Motivational surveys of the type discussed in chapter 4 provide the 'soft' measurement tools that allow the identification of low levels of motivation and commitment which deserve attention and resources. Focusing on these soft aspects avoids problems in the successful implantation of TQM as an holistic process.

Job design

A final aspect of designing a motivating organization is job design so that jobs are likely to interest and inspire employees. Chapters 5 and 6 outline this approach in more detail, suggesting that job redesign can improve productivity by as much as 16 per cent and can also bring about increases in job satisfaction.

In essence, job design arises from the idea that many people have a psychological need to extend their skill and competence. By designing jobs in a way that makes this growth possible an organization can encourage employees to become motivated by their job. The 'job characteristics' approach was pioneered by Hackman and Oldham (1975), who suggest that the job characteristics which motivate are (*see* chapter 3, p. 63):

1 Variety of work.
2 Working on an identifiable product (task identity).
3 Working on a task that has impact on others (task significance).
4 Autonomy.
5 Feedback on how the work is progressing.

Figure 25 on page 153 summarizes the key aspects of a motivating environment.

More detail of this approach is given in chapter 3. The main objective is to design jobs in a way that increases the job characteristics which motivate. However, some caution is needed before rushing headlong into a programme of job enrichment. The increases in motivation and satisfaction that can be gained by redesigning jobs are in some part dependent on the levels of growth need strength (GNS) of the employees concerned. Some individuals have a high GNS whereas others are relatively unconcerned about the opportunities for psychological growth offered by their jobs. Furthermore some jobs already offer a plethora of opportunities for psychological growth while other jobs are in need of enrichment and redesign. Before redesigning jobs, it is usually worth while checking the basic facts with a morale or motivation survey (*see* chapter 4). Surveys of morale and motivation need not be restricted to the kinds of factors identified by Hackman and Oldham. They can also be used to gauge satisfaction with factors such as pay, supervision and aspects of the organizational climate. The results of surveys have primary relevance to job design but they are also relevant to career structure, remuneration and appraisal. The use of surveys, plus groups specifically charged with examining the design of jobs (*see* chapter 5) can become a powerful method of bringing about planned organizational change.

Figure 27 identifies the organization and person factors that can be improved through job design. Symptoms suggesting problems with any of these factors could indicate that job redesign is appropriate, though some of the problems might be solved better by other means such as improvements in selection and placement, training, appraisal procedures or changes in pay.

Figure 27
Organization and person factors influenced by job design

Measuring motivation in individuals

Sometimes it is necessary to try to measure motivation in individual people. Usually this need arises in selection situations or where people are being considered as participants in some kind of motivational course. In fact, measures of an individual's level of motivation are probably the weakest link in a psychometrician's armoury. In part the weakness reflects the fact that psychometricians have devoted more attention to mental ability and personality. In part it reflects the relative instability of motivation. Intelligence and, to a lesser extent, personality are stable over a long period of years – especially when there, has not been a great change in the person's environment. In contrast, a person's motivation can vary quite dramatically over a period of weeks or even days. Despite these difficulties a number of measures of motivation have been constructed.

Probably the most widely researched measure is Rotter's (1966) Scale of the Locus of Control. It is based upon the idea that people have views on what determines the things that happen to them. *Externals* believe that their lives are determined by forces outside themselves. *Internals* believe that they themselves determine what happens to them. The presumption is that externals are more passive in relation to their environment and that, in contrast, internals will be motivated to activities which will shape their environment. Rotter's scale has been used extensively in research investigations. Despite the merit of being fairly short, it is not well suited to selection, since the questions are opaque and easy to manipulate.

Picture Story Exercises (PSE) are probably one of the most widely used measures of motivation in the area of work psychology. They are based on the ideas of McClelland, who is best known for his work on achievement motivation. McClelland's original work used the projective test known as the TAT (thematic apperception test). McClelland used four very vague pictures. Individuals looked briefly at each picture and then told a story about it: who the main characters were, what they were doing, what had led up to the situation, and what would follow. The pictures were so vague and were exposed so briefly that people had to fill in the details. In doing this they *projected* their own emotions on to the story they told. A strict scoring theme was devised, and the stories could

162

be scored according to how much of various themes had been projected into the stories (McClelland *et al*, 1953). Originally, stories were scored according to the amount of Achievement motivation they contained (nAch). Subsequent work focused upon the need for power (nPower) and the need for affiliation (nAff). These three needs were taken from a long list of needs developed by Murray (see Steers and Porter, 1979, pp 33–9). The PSE follow the same ideas but the actual pictures are more modern and more relevant to a business setting. The test seems particularly suitable for selection purposes because it is virtually impossible for candidates to divine the required responses. However, the strict scoring system, which requires well trained scorers, is time-consuming and unwieldy.

The MAT (Motivational Analysis Test) was developed by Cattell, the author of the 16PF Personality Test. It is a very sophisticated test which measures both motivational drives (ergs) and *sentiments*. The ergs represent the natural energy directed towards an objective. The sentiments are the energy we have learned by experience to devote to certain objectives. The ergs and sentiments measured by the MAT are:

Ergs	*sentiments*
Sex (mating)	Self-sentiment
Assertiveness	Super-ego (conscience)
Avoidance of danger	Career
Narcissism	Sweetheart/spouse
Destructive/Hostile	Home/parental

However, the MAT is a very sophisticated test and can be scored to give much more than scores on the five ergs and the five sentiments. The test measures each of these features in four different ways. Consequently it is able to estimate the conscious and the unconscious motivation in each area. This gives rise to another possibility – conflict scores. Someone whose unconscious motivation is much higher than their conscious motivation is likely to be in considerable motivational conflict! In many situations, a comparison of the conscious and unconscious levels of motivation can be illuminating in its own right. For example, if a 55 year old employee's conscious career motive was much higher than the unconscious career motive it could indicate a 'plateaued' employee who was once very interested in work but is now uninspired by it. This could be a useful signal for redeployment or job change. Merely feeding the finding back to the individual could be an important developmental activity in its own right.

Selection

Once an organization is structured in a way which has the potential to motivate employees, the next stage is to select employees who have the capacity to be motivated. Different employees are motivated to a different extent; unfortunately, selecting motivated employees is easier said than done. Interviews are relatively little help, because even the most unmotivated person can appear to be keen for the short duration of the interview. Furthermore there are very few valid psychological tests which measure motivation.

Probably the best test is the thematic apperception test, generally known as the TAT, described above. It can be used only by experienced psychologists and even in these circumstances there is some doubt about the accuracy of the results. A short test of achievement motivation is also available. Cattell's Motivation Analysis Test (*see* Cattell and Child, 1975) is designed to measure underlying differences in individual motivation, but although the test has promise there is little clear evidence that it taps a distinct set of motivators with any accuracy (Kline, 1983).

With school leavers it may sometimes be useful to measure a trait which is related to motivation interests. Many good interest tests exist. The Rothwell–Miller, the Kuder Vocational Interest Test and the Strong Vocational Interest Inventory are particularly well established. One of the drawbacks of using these tests is that, although they are very useful for vocational guidance, in a selection context their aims are very transparent and consequently they may be easy to fake.

Managers often rely on the traditional but less reliable interview to select employees who will be motivated. Some useful tips are:

1 Do not be over-influenced by the motivation or lack of it shown during the interview. Some people find it easy to act enthusiastically for an hour during the interview. Others feel threatened in an interview situation, and because they

'pull in their horns' they appear unmotivated whereas in the work situation they turn out to be keen workers.

2 Look for evidence of times when the candidate persisted longer than most people or where he or she achieved a high standard.

3 Research suggests that interviews which are structured and job-related (see Eder and Ferris, 1989; Dipboye, 1992) may be more accurate than normal interviews. One type of structured, job-related interview – the situational interview – involves the interviewer describing a series of work situations, derived from detailed job analysis, to applicants who are asked how they would react.

Training

Training and appraisal should run concurrently but, in the context of this book, they will be treated separately. Although many types of training are concerned largely with imparting new skills and knowledge, training is also well established as a method of changing people's attitudes and motives. At its simplest, training of this type consists of a sales conference in which a series of carefully chosen speakers seek to inspire the sales team with enthusiasm for the product, the company and themselves. Whether such conferences have any long term effect is not at all clear. In many situations the long term effect seems very short-lived. Except, perhaps, in new recruits the impact of such pep-talks is rapidly eroded under the workaday daily grind. The techniques adopted seem to be an amalgam of implied threat and the use of social esteem as a motive. Often the programme will include a session where participants are required publicly to commit themselves to certain targets, thus involving elements of goal-setting, competitiveness and self-esteem. This motivational technique is particularly useful when a quick boost is needed to encourage immediate action and reverse a decline.

For example, as Figure 28 shows, morale in unemployed executives tends to proceed through certain phases as unemployment continues. First there is an initial boost as the activity surrounding the first news of redundancy produces a short increase in morale. Problems then emerge, reality sets in and morale declines. Often a mood of pessimism develops

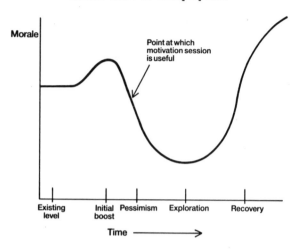

Figure 28
Morale curve in unemployment

and job-seeking activity declines. Sooner or later, however, old ideas are abandoned and the individual starts to try out new approaches. One new approach might be successful and this raises morale. In many situations a motivational talk or a motivational session can speed an individual through these phases by shortening the period of decline, increasing job-seeking activity and bringing forward the time of exploration of new ideas.

A more sophisticated use of training to increase motivation may have longer-lasting results. Over a longer period, and usually interspersed with other activities, training can be used to alter the expectancies and values of individuals. One of the first systematic approaches of this kind attempted to increase achievement motivation in executives. In this approach Alschuler *et al* (1970) developed a scheme where managers were taught to think, talk and act like highly achievement-motivated executives.

The expectancy-valence theory is particularly relevant to training designed to increase motivation. A programme can be produced which, using carefully arranged group discussion, or talks by role models, changes or influences participants' views about a reward which the company offers. Usually the reward is higher status, promotion or greater responsibility. Next, perhaps, by means of a talk using specific case

166

studies, it is stressed that the reward is given as a result of increased performance. Finally, participants take part in role-plays or more traditional training techniques which aim to clarify and consolidate the link between effort and performance.

For example, one programme designed to encourage more women into junior management started with a group discussion in which ostensibly the advantages and disadvantages of holding a managerial job were considered (Smith *et al*, 1984b). In practice the discussions were led by a skilful change agent; whilst she acknowledged the disadvantages she concentrated on the advantages of women in managerial careers and steered the discussion away from traditional forms of fulfilment. The initial changes in the value which participants placed on the rewards of a managerial job were increased and consolidated by talks from successful women managers who were briefed to emphasize positive aspects. The next stage was to emphasize the link between performance and reward, ie the reward of promotion came as a result of good performance as a supervisor. This was done by discussing three case studies in which competent women supervisors had discharged their duties in a very effective way and been duly promoted. The final and longest stage involved asking participants to estimate and discuss the effort needed to achieve the required levels of performance. It was supplemented by traditional training, such as sessions on time management, so that the personal effectiveness of participants might be increased.

Training in self-management, which incorporates the concepts of self-modelling (Dowrick and Hood, 1981) and self-efficacy (Bandura, 1982) discussed in chapter 2, can be an effective method of bringing about changes in values and attitudes. Training in self-management utilizes the principles of goal-setting to teach people self-observation, to compare their behaviour with relevant self-set goals, and to reward or punish themselves for continued commitment to attaining these self-set goals (Karoly and Kanfer, 1982). In an eight-week study designed to increase job attendance Frayne and Latham (1987) taught government employees how to manage personal and social obstacles to job attendance. Not only was there a subsequent increase in job attendance, but there was a corresponding increase in self-efficacy in being able to exercise influence over the employees' behaviour. A follow-up study with the same people was undertaken to determine the long-term effects of self-management training. Latham and Frayne (1989) found that the employees who had participated in the previous study still exhibited higher job attendance than the control group. This control group was then trained in self-management techniques. Three months later this second group showed the same increases in self-efficacy and job attendance as the original one.

Another training implication concerns the trainee's motivation in respect of the course itself. Expectancy-valence theory is relevant again here. Trainees must value the qualification obtained at the end of the training. Trainees must also believe that if they complete the training successfully they will be offered a job. Training conducted within a company rarely encounters problems of this kind but government-sponsored schemes, especially those for youths, can run into difficulties. Often less than 40 per cent of participants on these schemes obtain suitable places at the end of training. This is too low a proportion for the schemes to have a noticeable motivating effect. Similar problems can be encountered by some educational courses. Trainees should feel that if they work hard they will succeed in obtaining the qualification offered. 'Pass' rates must be sufficiently high to strengthen the link between effort and performance, but at the same time they must not be so low that success is devalued because 'even fools can pass'.

Appraisal

Appraisal systems have many purposes. In motivational terms one of the most important aspects of appraisal sessions is to set (in collaboration with the person concerned) appropriate goals for achievement. Locke's goal-setting approach to motivation was outlined in chapter 2, and it was noted that goal-setting is one of the most effective ways of increasing performance. It follows that appraisal sessions should set clear, specific goals which the person appraised considers fair and has helped to set.

Participation in goal-setting is very important. If hard goals are imposed on employees they are likely to be rejected, and when goals are rejected they have little influence on actual performance. On the other hand, if the goals are accepted, difficult goals lead to better performance than easy goals.

However, encouraging participation does not mean complete freedom: targets should be arrived at by a process of sensible discussion. In the context of this section individual goals are usually set during an appraisal session. In situations where goals are needed for groups of workers, other procedures will be used.

There are strong links between self-efficacy, motivation and goal-setting. Self-efficacy is a person's view of how well he or she is able to execute required actions. Higher self-efficacy tends to be related to higher performance. Appraisal sessions can play a useful role in building up individuals' views of their own competence and thus lead them to strive for, and often achieve, more difficult goals.

A second way in which appraisal interviews can be used to motivate employees is to communicate the links which exist between effort and performance (E → P). (*See* chapter 2 for an explanation of expectancy-valence theory.) A skilfully conducted appraisal session should be able to establish whether an employee expects that increased effort will lead to better performance. Some subordinates fail to try harder because they do not believe the extra effort produces better results. Once this is detected, counselling and the discussion of positive examples can produce greater effort. However, ethical standards must be maintained. Skilful manipulation could lead an employee into false beliefs. Expectancies play a crucial part in the motivation of individuals and there is no reason to believe that they are the same in all employees. Different groups, ethnic subgroups, males, females may have different expectancies. The appraisal situation provides a golden opportunity to discuss the expectancies held by individual employees. The information gained can be used, in counselling, to correct misapprehensions but it can also be used to identify aspects of the organization, such as promotion procedures, which need to be altered so that motivation is increased.

A third use of appraisal interviews in motivation is to strengthen the belief in a link between performance and reward (P → O). An employee may be convinced that extra effort will produce better performance but may not believe that the superior performance will be rewarded. Again, counselling and the citation of examples can help to create beliefs which are more conducive to higher motivation. However, cynical manipulation of employees' expectations should be avoided for both practical and ethical reasons. In the long term an employee whose expectations have been raised and then left unfulfilled is likely to become highly demotivated. In the final analysis a crucial determinant of $E \rightarrow P$ and $P \rightarrow O$ expectancies is what actually happens (ie feedback). If feedback demonstrates that performance does *not* lead to high valence rewards, motivation will suffer. The importance of feedback for good performance is crucial. As expectancy–valence theory suggests, feedback provides the basis of people's expectancies concerning the links between effort, performance and reward. Feedback to individuals must be clear, informative and direct. If a tennis player cannot see where the ball is landing on the other side of the net, feedback is low, and the development of skill and high levels of performance will also be low.

Another use of appraisal sessions is to establish the rewards which an employee values. Individuals are motivated by different things. It is therefore wrong to assume that everyone is motivated by pay. It is also commonly assumed that most people are motivated by the prospect of promotion and, at the drop of a hat, sociologists and psychologists assume that job enrichment is at the top of everyone's list of priorities. Because of these assumptions, resources are wasted in offering employees rewards which they value only marginally. Often the identification of an individual's goals and values can lead to discussion of how the goals can be met. For example, if it was revealed that the job lacked variety, identity and autonomy, the remainder of the appraisal session could be devoted to finding ways of enriching it.

Research on the structure and content of appraisal interviews (Nemeroff and Wexley, 1979) has established a link between what takes place during appraisal interviews and the satisfaction and motivation to improve of the person who has been appraised. In the Nemeroff and Wexley study, satisfaction on the part of the interviewee was greater when the interviewer:

1 Behaved in a friendly fashion.
2 Ended on a positive note.
3 Scheduled a follow-up meeting.
4 Praised people for good work.

Motivation to improve was higher when the interviewer:

1 Invited the participant to participate in goal-setting.
2 Invited the participant to state his or her own position concerning problems, etc.
3 Asked for the participant's view on how he or she was doing.
4 Asked about specific problems.

Remuneration

In chapter 5 it was pointed out that remuneration can be used as an effective way of motivating employees. However, this does not mean that offering money always increases motivation: some employees do not value money and the compensation package may be assembled in such a way that it fails to motivate.

In many cases, wages do not act as a motivator because performance is not linked to rewards. For example, in the majority of jobs pay is linked to seniority and length of service rather than efficiency and effort. This is certainly true of jobs in government service, and it is very often true in private industry. In general, both the good and the poor performer receive the same yearly increment. Even incentive schemes and piece-rate schemes are unlikely to attain the full motivational impact, because they are constrained by other factors. One of these factors concerns group norms of productivity. Very early experiments in industry show that each group of workers establishes a fairly narrow band of acceptable production. Anyone who allows his production to exceed this level will be subjected to pressure to conform and may be labelled a rate-buster. The nature of the work also imposes constraints which militate against the full motivational impact of financial rewards. Often performance is limited by factors outside the control of the individual, such as the speed of a conveyor belt or the rate at which customers enter a shop.

In the face of these and other difficulties many organizations settle for establishing a rate for the job which is paid to all the holders of the job concerned. However, from the motivational viewpoint even this decision is fraught with difficulty. The rate which is used will have an effect on the motivation of employees. In chapter 2 the equity theory of motivation was outlined. According to equity theory, employees balance what they put into a job with what they receive from it. If the inputs and rewards do not balance, people try to make them equal by changing the degree of effort they put into their work. Thus, according to equity theory, if the remuneration is too low employees work less. If the remuneration is too high they will try harder in order to match their employer's generosity. Unfortunately, the results of actual experiments give only partial support to the predictions derived from equity theory. In general it is true that, when remuneration is poor, workers put less effort into their job but it is far less clear whether overpaying results in increased productivity.

Conclusion

None of the approaches to motivation supports the view that everyone should be treated the same. They do stress, however, that people need to be treated fairly and, above all, to *perceive* that they are being treated fairly. When utilizing the ideas discussed in this chapter to enhance motivation and performance, equality presents a major practical difficulty. It is perhaps possible, without too much difficulty, to ensure that job holders feel they are getting appropriate outputs (pay, praise, promotion, etc). The theories discussed, however, suggest that these outputs should differ from person to person to take account of individual preference. Problems arise when one person compares his or her treatment with that of someone else. Who is the appropriate person for comparison? How does one outcome, such as a financial bonus, compare with another, such as extra time off? The answer to these questions of course will vary from person to person. Arriving at a strategy that provides individual motivation, catering for individual differences and yet appearing equitable to all employees is a major challenge. The ideas outlined in this chapter and elaborated in the previous chapters show how the challenge can be met.

The motivation of employees should be of vital concern to all managers. It is no easy responsibility, since individuals differ in what motivates them. The situation is complicated by the fact that motivation is not a simple phenomenon, and several theories are needed to account for even the basic facts.

Nevertheless, by applying these theories to designing organizations, implementing Total Quality Management systems, selection, training, appraisal and remuneration, a great deal of progress can be made.

References

ACKOFF, Russell, and EMERY, Fred E. *On purposeful systems*. Trowbridge, Tavistock, 1972

ADAMS, J S. 'Inequality in social exchange' in Leonard BERKOWITZ, (ed.), *Advances in experimental social psychology*, 2. New York, Academic Press, 1965

ALDERFER, Clayton P. *Existence, relatedness and growth: human needs in organizational settings*. New York, Free Press, 1972

ALGERA, Jen A. ' "Objective" and perceived task characteristics as a determinant of reactions by task performers', *Journal of Occupational Psychology*, Vol 56, No 2, 1983, pp 95–107

ALGERA, Jen A. 'Feedback systems in organizations', in C L COOPER and I T ROBERTSON (eds), '*International Review of Industrial and Organizational Psychology*, 1990, pp 169–94

ALSCHULER, Alfred S, *et al. Teaching achievement motivation*. Middletown, Conn., Educational Ventures, 1970

ANDREWS, J D W. 'The achievement motive and advancement in two types of organizations', *Journal of Personality and Social Psychology*, Vol 6, 1967, pp 163–9

ANNETT, J *et al. Task analysis*. Department of Employment. Training Information Paper 6. London, HMSO, 1971

ARGYRIS, C. 'Personality vs organization', *Organizational Dynamics*, Vol 3, No 2, 1974, pp 2–17

ARNOLD, H J, and HOUSE, R J. 'Methodological and substantive extensions to the job characteristics model of motivation', *Organizational Behaviour and Human Performance*, Vol 25, 1980, pp 161–83

ARVEY, R D, and IVANCEVICH, J M. 'Punishment in organizations: a review, propositions and research suggestions', *Academy of Management Review*, Vol 5, 1980, pp 123–32

ASHFORD, S J. 'Self-assessments in organizations: a literature review and integrative model', in B M STAW and L L CUMMINGS (eds), *Research in organizational behaviour*, Vol 11, pp 133–74. Greenwich, Conn: JAI Press, 1989

ASHFORD, S J, and CUMMINGS, L L. 'Feedback as an individual resource: personal strategies of creating information', *Organizational Behaviour and Human Performance*, Vol 32, 1983, pp 370–98.

ATKINSON, P E. *Creating culture change: the key to successful Total Quality Management*. Kempston, IFS, 1990

AUSTIN, J T, and BOBKO, P. 'Goal setting theory: unexplored areas and future research needs', *Journal of Occupational Psychology* Vol 58, 1985, pp 289–308

AVERGOLD, M . 'Swedish experiments in industrial democracy', in Louis E DAVIS and Albert B CHERNS (eds). *The quality of working life: cases and commentary*. New York, Free Press, 1975

BABCHUCK, N, and GOODE, W J. 'Work incentives in a self-determined group', *American Sociological Review*, Vol 16, 1951, pp 679–87

BAGCHUS, P M, and VAN DOOREN, F J P. 'The Management of organizations', in DRENTH, P J D *et al. Handbook of work and organisational psychology*. Chichester, Wiley, 1984

BANDURA, A. *Social learning theory*. Englewood Cliffs, N.J., Prentice Hall, 1977

BANDURA, A. 'Self-efficacy mechanism in human agency', *American Psychologist*, Vol 37, 1982, pp 122–47

BANDURA, Albert. 'Self-regulation of motivation and action through goal-systems', in V Hamilton *et al*. (eds), *Cognitive perspectives on emotion and motivation*. Dordrecht, Kluwer Academic, 1988

BANDURA, Albert and CERVONE, D. 'Self-evaluative and self-efficacy mechanisms governing the effects of goal systems', *Journal of Personality and Social Psychology*, Vol 45, 1983, pp 1017–28

BEDEIAN, A G. *Organizations: theory and analysis*. Hinsdale, Ill., Dryden Press, 1980

BENDIX, R. *Work and authority in industry*. New York, Wiley, 1956

BLACKLER, F H M, and BROWN, C A. *Job redesign and management control: studies in British Leyland and Volvo*. Westmead, Saxon House, 1978

BLANDY, Auriol. 'Suffolk area ambulance service', *in* WORK RESEARCH UNIT, *Meeting the challenge of change: case studies*. London, WRU, 1982

BLAU, P M. *The dynamics of bureaucracy*. Chicago, University of Chicago Press, 1955

BLAUNER, Robert. *Alienation and freedom: the factory worker and his industry*. Chicago, University of Chicago Press, 1964

BLUM, Milton L, and NAYLOR, James C. *Industrial psychology*, 3rd edn. New York, Harper and Row, 1968

BOADEN, Ruth J, *et al*. 'The management of quality within a major bank', *Proceedings of the Workshop on Quality Management in Services*. European Institute for Advanced Studies in Management. Brussels, 1991, pp 371–90.

BOTTERILL, M. 'Why you should implement TQ', *Management Services*, 18–21 December, 1991

BOWERS, David G. 'OD techniques and their results in 23 organizations: the Michigan ICL study', *Journal of Applied Behavioral Science*, Vol 9, No 1, 1973, pp 21–43

BOWERS, David G, and FRANKLIN, Jerome L. *Survey-guided development, 1, Data-based organizational change*, rev. edn. La Jolla, Cal., University Associates, 1977

BRAND, D D, *et al*. 'Improving white-collar productivity at HUD', in Richard M O'BRIEN *et al* (eds), *Industrial behavior modification: a learning-based approach to industrial-organizational problems*. New York, Pergamon, 1982

BRIGHT, K. 'Can maturity in Total Quality Management be defined in terms of organizational culture?' MSc thesis, School of Management, UMIST, Manchester, 1991

BUCHANAN, David A, and BODDY, David. 'Advanced technology and the quality of working life: the effects of word-processing on video typists', *Journal of Occupational Psychology*, Vol 55, No 1, 1982, pp 1–11

BUCHANAN, David A, and BODDY, David. 'Advanced technology and the quality of working life: the effects of computerized controls on biscuit-making operations', *Journal of Occupational Psychology*, Vol 56, No 2, 1983, p 109–19

BURNS, Tom, and STALKER, G M. *The management of innovation*. London, Tavistock, 1961

BUTTERISS, M. *The quality of working life: the expanding international scene*. Work Research Unit Paper 5. London, Work Research Unit, 1975

CAMERON, S. *Organization change: a description of alternative strategies*. Work Reseach Unit Occasional Paper 5. London, Work Research Unit, 1973.

CAMPBELL, D J. 'Task complexity: a review and analysis', *Academy of Management Review*, Vol. 13, 1988, pp 40–52

CAMPBELL, J P, *et al*. *Managerial behavior, performance and effectiveness*. New York, McGraw-Hill, 1970

CAMPION, M A, and LORD, R G. 'A control systems conceptualization of the goal-setting and changing process', *Organizational Behaviour and Human Performance*, Vol 30, 1982, pp 265–87

CAMPION, M A, and THAYER, P W. 'Development and field evaluation of an interdisciplinary measure of job design', *Journal of Applied Psychology*, Vol 70, 1985, pp 29–43

CARBY, Keith. *Job design in practice*. London, Institute of Personnel Management, 1976

CARVER, C S, and SCHEIER, M F. *Attention and self-regulation: a control theory approach to human behaviour*. New York, Springer-Verlag, 1981

CARVER, C S, and SCHEIER, M F. 'Control theory: a useful conceptual framework for personality, social, clinical and health psychology', *Psychological Bulletin*, Vol 92, 1982, pp 111–35

CATTELL, R B, and CHILD, D. *Motivation and dynamic structure*. London, Holt-Rinehart and Winston, 1975

CENTRAL STATISTICAL OFFICE. *Social trends*. London, 1973

CHAMPOUX, J E. 'A multivariate test of the job characteristics theory of work motivation', *Journal of Organizational Behavior*, Vol 12, 1991, pp 431–46

CHILD, J. *Organization: a guide to problems and practice*, 2nd edn. Harper & Row, London, 1987

COCHRAN, W. C. *Sampling techniques*. London, Wiley, 1963

COLLARD, R. *Total Quality: success through people*. IPM, London, 1989

COOK, John D, et al. *The experience of work: a compendium and review of 249 measures and their uses*. London, Academic Press, 1981

COOPER, Cary L. 'Employee participation and improving the quality of work life' in TORRINGTON, D (ed). *Industrial Relations in Europe*. London, Associated Business Press, 1977

COOPER, M. Dominic, et al. 'Assigned or participatively set goals: do they make a difference?', paper presented at the British Psychological Society Occupational Psychology Conference, Liverpool, January 1992

COOPER, Robert. 'Task characteristics and intrinsic motivation', *Human Relations*, Vol 26, August 1973, pp 387–408

COOPER, Robert. *Job motivation and job design*. London, Institute of Personnel Management, 1974

CROSBY, P B. *Quality is free*. New York, McGraw-Hill, 1979

CROSS, Denys. 'The worker opinion survey: a measure of shop-floor satisfaction', *Occupational Psychology*, Vol 47, Nos 3–4, 1973, pp 193–208

CYERT, Richard, and MARCH, J G. *A behavioral theory of the firm*. Englewood Cliffs, N.J., Prentice Hall, 1963

DALE, B G, and PLUNKETT, J J (eds). *Managing quality*. Hemel Hempstead, Philip Allan, 1990

DAVIS, Louis E. 'The design of jobs', *Industrial Relations*, Vol 6, 1966, pp 21–5

DAVIS, Louis E. 'Evolving alternative organization designs: their sociotechnical bases', *Human Relations*, Vol 30, No 3, 1977, pp 261–73

DAVIS, Louis E, and TAYLOR, James C. 'Technology, effects on job, work and organizational structure: a contingency view', in Louis E DAVIS and Albert B CHERNS (eds). *The quality of working life*. New York, Free Press, 1975

DAVIS, S M, and LAWRENCE, P R. *Matrix*. Reading, Mass., Addison-Wesley. 1977

DAVIS, T R V, and LUTHANS, F. 'A social learning approach to organizational behaviour', *Academy of Management Review*, Vol 5, 1980, pp 281–90

DEMING, W E. *Out of the crisis*, Cambridge, Mass., MIT Press, 1986

DIPBOYE, R L. *Selection interviews: process perspectives*. Cincinatti, Southwestern Publishing, 1992

DOWRICK, P W, and HOOD, M. 'Comparison of self-modelling and small cash incentives in a sheltered workshop', *Journal of Applied Psychology*. Vol 66, 1981, pp 394–7

DUBIN, R. 'Supervision and Productivity' in R. DUBIN et al, *Leadership and Productivity*. San Francisco, Chandler, 1965

DUMAS, R A. 'Organizational quality: how to avoid common pitfalls', *Quality Progress*, May 1989, pp 41–4

EDER, R W, and FERRIS, G R. *The employment interview: theory, research, and practice*. London, Sage, 1989

ELLUL, Jacques. *The technological society*. New York, Vintage Books, 1964

EMERY, Fred E. *Characteristics of socio-technical systems*. London, Tavistock Institute of Human Relations, Document 527, 1959

EMERY, Fred E. 'Designing socio-technical systems for "greenfield" sites', *Journal of Occupational Behaviour*, Vol 1, No 1, 1980, pp 19–27

EREZ, Miriam. 'Feedback: a necessary condition for the goal- setting performance relationship', *Journal of Occupational Psychology*, Vol 62, No 5, 1977, pp 624–7

EREZ, Miriam. 'Expectancy theory predictions of willingness to be retrained: the case of ratings advancement in the Israeli merchant navy', *Journal of Occupational Psychology*, Vol 52, No 1, 1979, pp 35–40

EREZ, Miriam, and ZIDON, Isaac. 'Effect of good acceptance on the relationship of goal difficulty to performance', *Journal of Applied Psychology*, Vol 69, No 1, 1984, pp 69–78

FEIGENBAUM, A V. *Total quality control*, 3rd edn. New York, McGraw-Hill, 1983

FEIN, M. 'Job enrichment: a re-evaluation' in Richard M STEERS and Lyman W PORTER (eds). *Motivation and work behavior*, 2nd edn. New York, McGraw-Hill, 1979

FINE, Sidney A, and WILEY, Wretha W. 'An introduction to functional job analysis', in Edwin A FLEISHMAN and Alan R BASS (eds), *Studies in personnel and industrial psychology*, 3rd edn. Homewood, Ill., Dorsey, 1974

FINEMAN, S. 'The achievement motive construct and its measurement: where are we now?' *British Journal of Psychology*, Vol 68, 1977, 1–22

FORD, Robert N. *Motivation through work itself*. New York, American Management Association, 1969

FRAYNE, C A, and LATHAM, Gary P. 'Application of social learning theory to employee self-management of attendance', *Journal of Applied Psychology*, Vol 72, 1987, pp 387–92

FRENCH, J R P, and CAPLAN, R D. 'Organizational stress and individual strain', in A J MARROW (ed), *The failure of success*. New York, AMACOM, 1973

FRIED, Y, and FERRIS, G R. 'The validity of the job characteristics model: a review and meta-analysis', *Personnel Psychology*, Vol 40, 1987, 287–322

GALBRAITH, J R. *Organizational design*. Reading, Mass., Addison-Wesley. 1977

GARLAND, Howard. 'Relation of effort–performance expectancy to performance in goal-setting experiments', *Journal of Applied Psychology*, Vol 69, No 1, 1984, pp 79–84

GARVIN, D A. 'Quality on the line, *Harvard Business Review*, Vol 61, 1983, pp 65–75

GERHART, B. 'Sources of variance in incumbent perceptions of job complexity', *Journal of Applied Psychology*, Vol 73, 1988, pp 154–62

GOUGH, H G. 'A managerial potential scale for the California Psychological Inventory', *Journal of Applied Psychology*, Vol 69, 1984, pp 233–40

GOULDNER, A W. *Patterns of industrial democracy*. Glencoe, Ill., Free Press, 1954

GRAY, J. 'The myth of the myths about B.Mod. in organizations', *Academy of Management Review*, Vol 4, 1979, pp 121–9

GREENBERG, J. 'A taxonomy of organizational justice theories', *Academy of Management Review*, Vol 12, 1987, pp 9–22

GREENBERG, J. 'Reactions to procedural injustice in payment systems: do the ends justify the means?' *Journal of Applied Psychology*, Vol 75, 1987a, pp 55–61

GREENBERG, J. 'Employee theft as a reaction to underpayment inequity: the hidden costs of pay cuts', *Journal of Applied Psychology*, Vol 75, 1990, pp 561–8

GROONROOS, C. *Strategic management and marketing in the service sector*. Bromley, Chartwell-Bratt, 1984

GULICK, Luther H, and URWICK, Lydell, (eds). *Papers on the science of administra-*

tion. New York, Columbia University Press, 1937

GULOWSEN, Jon. 'A measure of work group autonomy', in Louis E DAVIS and C James TAYLOR (eds), *Design of jobs.* Harmondsworth, Penguin, 1972

GYLLENHAMMAR, Pehr G. 'How Volvo adapts work to people', in Richard M STEERS and Lyman W PORTER (eds). *Motivation and work behavior,* 2nd edn, New York, McGraw-Hill, 1979

HACKMAN, J Richard. 'Towards understanding the role of tasks in behavioral research', *Acta Psychologica,* Vol 31, 1969, pp 97–128

HACKMAN, J Richard. 'Work design' in J Richard HACKMAN and J L SUTTLE (eds), *Improving life at work: behavioral science approaches to organizational change.* Santa Monica, Cal., Goodyear, 1977

HACKMAN, J Richard. 'Work design', in Richard M STEERS and Lyman W PORTER (eds), *Motivation and work behavior,* 2nd edn. New York, McGraw-Hill, 1979

HACKMAN J Richard. 'Changing views of motivation in work groups', in K D DUNCAN *et al.* (eds), *Changes in working life.* Chichester, Wiley, 1980

HACKMAN, J Richard, and LAWLER, Edward E. 'Employee reactions to job characteristics', *Journal of Applied Psychology,* Vol 55, No 3, 1971, pp 259–86

HACKMAN, J Richard, and OLDHAM, G R. *The Job Diagnostic Survey: an instrument for the diagnosis of jobs and the evaluation of job redesign projects.* New Haven, Conn., Yale University Press 1974

HACKMAN, J Richard, and OLDHAM, G R. 'Development of the job diagnostic survey', *Journal of Applied Psychology,* Vol 60, No 2, 1975, pp 159–70

HACKMAN, J Richard, and OLDHAM G R. 'Motivation through the design of work: test of a theory', *Organizational Behavior and Human Performance,* Vol 16, No 2, 1976, pp 250–79

HACKMAN, J Richard, and OLDHAM, G R. *Work redesign.* New York, Addison-Wesley, 1980

HALL, D T, and NOUGAIM, K E. 'An examination of Maslow's need hierarchy in the organizational setting', *Organizational Behavior and Human Performance,* Vol 3, No 1, 1968, pp 12–35

HAMNER, W C and E P. 'Behavior modification on the bottom line', *Organizational Dynamics,* Vol 3, spring 1976, pp 3–21

HANDY, Charles B. *Understanding organizations.* Harmondsworth, Penguin, 1976

HELLRIEGAL, D, *et al. Organizational behavior,* 5th edn. St Paul, Minn., West Publishing, 1989

HENDRICKS, C F, and TRIPLETT, A. 'TQM: strategy for 1990s management', *Personnel Administrator,* Vol 34, 1989, pp 42–8

HENGEN, William K. 'Change processes within organizations', in David BIRCHALL and Barbara MORRIS (eds). *The practice of job design and work organization: ideas and issues.* Henley on Thames, Administrative Staff College, Work Research Group, 1978

HEROLD, D M, and PARSONS, C K. 'Assessing the feedback environment in work organizations: development of the Job Feedback Survey, *Journal of Applied Psychology,* Vol 70, 1985, pp 290–305

HERZBERG, F. 'One more time: how do you motivate employees?' *Harvard Business Review,* January–February 1968, pp 53–62

HILL, Stephen. 'How do you manage a flexible firm? The Total Quality model', *Work, Employment and Society,* Vol 5, No 3, 1991, pp 397–415

HOLLENBECK, J R, *et al.* 'An empirical examination of the antecedents of commitment to difficult goals', *Journal of Applied Psychology,* Vol 74, 1989, pp 18–23

HUNTER, J E, *et al. Meta-analysis: cumulating research findings across studies.* Beverly Hills, Cal., Sage, 1982

ILGEN, D R, NEBEKER, D, and PRITCHARD, R. 'Expectancy theory measures: an empirical comparison in an experimental simulation', *Organizational Behaviour and Human Performance,* Vol 21, 1981, pp 189–223

IMADA, A S, and ROBERTSON, M M. 'Cultural perspectives in participatory ergonomics', *Proceedings of the Human Factors Society*, 31st annual meeting, 1987, pp 1018–22

INDIK, P. 'Organizational size and member participation: some empirical tests of alternative explanations', *Human Relations*, Vol 18, 1965, pp 339–22

ISHIKAWA, K. *What is Total Quality Control? The Japanese way*, Prentice-Hall, Englewood Cliffs, 1985

JAMES, Lawrence R, and JONES, A P. 'Organizational climate: a review of theory and research', *Psychological Bulletin*, Vol 81, 1974, pp 1096–112

JAMES, Lawrence R, and JONES, A P. 'Organizational structure: a review of structural dimensions and their conceptual relationships with individual attitudes and behaviour', *Organizational Behavior and Human Performance*, Vol 16, 1976, pp 74–113

JAMES, Lawrence R, et al. 'Psychological climate: implication from cognitive social learning theory and interactional psychology', *Personnel Psychology*, Vol 31, No 4, 1978, pp 783–813

JONES, A P, and JAMES, Lawrence R. 'Psychological climate: dimensions and relationships of individual and aggregated work environment perceptions', *Organizational Behavior and Human Performance*, Vol 23, 1979, pp 201–50

JURAN, J M (ed). *Quality control handbook*, 3rd edn, New York, McGraw-Hill, 1979

JURAN, J M (ed). *Quality control handbook*, 4th edn. New York, McGraw-Hill, 1988

KANFER, Ruth. 'Work motivation: new directions in theory and research', in C L COOPER and I T ROBERTSON (eds), *International Review of Industrial and Organizational Psychology*, 1992

KAROLY, P, and KANFER, F H. *Self-management and behaviour change: from theory to practice*. New York, Pergamon Press, 1982

KATZ, D, and KAHN, R L. *The social psychology of organizations*. New York, Wiley, 1966

KATZ, Daniel, and KAHN, Robert Luis. *The social psychology of organizations*, 2nd edn. Chichester, Wiley, 1978

KAZDIN, A E. *Behavior modification in applied settings*, rev. edn. Homewood, Ill., Dorsey, 1980

KEMP, Nigel J, et al. 'Autonomous work groups in a greenfield site: a comparative study', *Journal of Occupational Psychology*, Vol 56, No 4, 1983, pp 271–88

KERNON, M C, and LORD, R G. 'Effects of valence, expectancies, and goal-performance discrepancies in single and multiple goal environments', *Journal of Applied Psychology*, Vol 75, 1990, pp 194–203

KIGGUNDU, M N. 'Task independence and job design: test of a theory', *Organizational Behavior and Human Performance*, Vol 31, 1983, pp 145–72

KLEIN, H J. 'An integrated control theory model of work motivation', *Academy of Management Review*, Vol 14, 1989, pp 150–72

KLEIN, L. 'Some problems of theory and method', in Reginald G SELL and Patricia SHIPLEY (eds), *Satisfaction in work design: ergonomics and other approaches*. London, Taylor and Francis, 1979

KLINE, P. *Personality: Measurement and Theory*. London, Hutchinson, 1983

KOTTER, John P. *Organizational dynamics: diagnosis and intervention*. Reading, Mass., Addison-Wesley, 1978

KREJCIE, R V, and MORGAN, D W. 'Determining sample size for research activities', *Educational and Psychological Measurement*, Vol 30, 1970, pp 607–10

LASCELLES, D M, and DALE, B G. 'Quality management: the chief executive's perception and role', *European Journal of Management*, Vol 8, No 1, 1990, pp 67–75

LATHAM, Gary P, and FRAYNE, C A. 'Self-management training for increasing job attendance: a follow-up and replication', *Journal of Applied Psychology*, Vol 74, 1989, pp 411–16

LATHAM, G P, et al, 'Resolving scientific disputes by the joint design of crucial experiments by the antagonists', *Journal of Applied Psychology*, Vol 73, 1988, pp

753–72

LAWLER, Edward E. 'Control systems in organizations' in Marvin D DUNNETTE (ed), *Handbook of industrial and organizational psychology*. Chicago, Rand McNally, 1976

LAWLER, Edward E, and PORTER, Lyman W. 'Antecedent attitudes of effective managerial performance', *Organizational Behavior and Human Performance*, Vol 2, 1967, pp 122–42

LAWLER, Edward E, and RHODE, J G. *Information and control in organizations*. Pacific Palisades, Cal., Goodyear, 1976

LAWRENCE, P R, and LORSCH, J W. 'Differentiation and integration in complex organizations', *Administrative Science Quarterly*, Vol 12, 1967, pp 1–47

LEAVITT, H J, et al. . *Readings in managerial psychology*, 3rd edn. Chicago, University of Chicago Press, 1980

LEVITT, T. 'Marketing success through differentiation of anything', *Harvard Business Review*, January–February. 1980

LEWIN, Kurt. *Field theory in social science*. New York, Harper and Row, 1951

LIKERT, Rensis. *New patterns of management*. New York, McGraw-Hill, 1961

LOCKE, Edwin A. 'Toward a theory of task motivation and incentives', *Organizational Behavior and Human Performance*, Vol 3, 1968, pp 157–89

LOCKE, Edwin A. 'The myths of behavior modification in organizations', *Academy of Management Review*, Vol 4, 1977, pp 543–53

LOCKE, E A, and BRYAN, J F. 'Grade goals as determinants of academic achievement', *Journal of General Psychology*, Vol 79, 1968, pp 217–28

LOCKE, E A, and LATHAM, G P. *A theory of goal setting and task performance*. London, Prentice-Hall, 1990

LOCKE, Edwin A et al. 'An experimental case study of the successes and failures of job enrichment in a government agency', *Journal of Applied Psychology*, Vol 61, No 6, 1976, pp 701–11

LOCKE, Edwin A, et al. 'The relative effectiveness of four methods of motivating employee performance', paper presented at the NATO International Conference on Changes in the Nature and Quality of Working Life. New York, Wiley, 1979

LOCKE, Edwin A, et al. 'Goal setting and task performance, 1969–1980', *Psychological Bulletin*, Vol 90, 1981, pp 125–52

LOCKE, Edwin A, et al. 'Effect of self-efficacy, goals and task strategies on task performance', *Journal of Applied Psychology*, Vol 69, No 2, 1984, pp 241–51

LOCKE, Edwin A, et al. 'Using self-efficacy theory to resolve the conflict between goal-setting theory and expectancy theory in organizational behaviour and industrial/organizational psychology', *Journal of Social and Clinical Psychology*, Vol 4, 1986, pp 328–38

LOCKE, Edwin A, et al. 'Separating the effects of goal specificity from goal level', *Organizational Behavior and Human Decision Processes*, Vol 43, 1989, pp 270–87

LORSCH, J W, et al. *Understanding management*. New York, Harper, 1978

LUPTON, T, and TANNER, I. 'Work design in Europe, in K D DUNCAN, et al., *Changes in working life*. Chichester, Wiley, 1980

LUTHANS, Fred, and KREITNER, Robert. *Organizational behavior modification*. Glenview, Ill., Scott-Foresman, 1975

MCCLELLAND, David C, and BOYATZIS, Richard E. 'Leadership motive pattern and long-term success in management', *Journal of Applied Psychology*, Vol 67, 1982, pp 737–43

MCCLELLAND, D C, et al. *The achievement motive*. New York, Appleton Century Croft, 1953

McGREGOR, Douglas. *The human side of enterprise*. New York, McGraw-Hill, 1960

MAHONEY, T A, and FROST, P J. 'The role of technology in organizational effectiveness', *Organizational Behavior and Human Performance*, Vol II, 1974, pp 122–38

MAMBREY, P., et al. 'Experiences in participative systems design', in P. DOH-

ERTY *et al.* (eds), *System design for human development and productivity: participation and beyond*, pp 345–58. Amsterdam, North-Holland, 1987

MANSFIELD, R. 'Formal and informal structure/, in M GRUNEBERG and T WALL (eds), *Social psychology and organizational behaviour*. Chichester, Wiley, 1984

MASLOW, A H. *Motivation and personality*, 2nd edn. New York, Harper, 1970

MAYO, Elton. *The social problem of an industrial civilization*. Cambridge, Mass., Harvard University Press, 1945

MERTON, Robert K. *Social theory and social structure*. Glencoe, Ill., Free Press, 1957

MILLER, G A, *et al. Plans and the structure of behavior*. New York, Holt, 1960

MIRVIS, Philip H, and LAWLER, Edward E. 'Measuring the financial impact of employee attitudes', *Journal of Applied Psychology*, Vol 62, No 1, 1977, pp 1–8

MOSER, C A, and KALTON. G. *Survey methods in social investigation*, 2nd edn. London, Heinemann, 1971

NADLER, D A. 'The effects of feedback on task group behaviour: a review of the experimental research', *Organizational Behavior and Human Peformance*, Vol 23, 1979, pp 309–38

NADLER, D A, and LAWLER, Edward E. 'Motivation: a diagnostic approach', in Richard M STEERS and Lyman W PORTER (eds), *Motivation and work behavior*, 2nd edn. New York, McGraw-Hill, 1979

NAYLOR, J C, *et al.* 'Goal setting: a theoretical analysis of a motivational technology', in B M STAW and L L CUMMINGS (eds), *Research in Organizational Behaviour*, Vol 6, pp 95–140. Greenwich, Conn., JAI Press. 1980

NEMEROFF, Wayne F, and WEXLEY, Kenneth N. 'An exploration of the relationships between performance feedback interview characteristics and interview outcomes as perceived by managers and subordinates', *Journal of Occupational Psychology*, Vol 52, No 1, 1979, pp 25–34

NIE, N H, *et al. SPSS: Statistical Package for the Social Sciences*. New York, McGraw-Hill, 1975

NUTTIN, J. *Motivation, planning and action*. Hillsdale, N.J., Erlbaum, 1984

O'BRIEN, Richard M, *et al.* (eds), *Industrial behavior modification: a learning-based approach to industrial organizational problems*. New York, Pergamon, 1982

OAKLAND, J. *Total Quality Management*. London, Heinemann, 1989

OLDHAM, Greg R, and HACKMAN, J Richard. 'Relationships between organizational structure and employee reactions: comparing alternative frameworks', *Administrative Science Quarterly*, Vol 26, 1981, pp 66–83

OLDHAM, Greg R, *et al. Norms for the Job Diagnostic Survey*. Yale University School of Organization and Management, Technical report 16, 1978

ORPEN, Christopher. 'The effects of job enrichment on employee satisfaction, motivation, involvement and performance: a field experiment', *Human Relations*, Vol 32, No 3, 1979, pp 189–217

O'TOOLE, James. *Work in America*. Boston, Mass., MIT Press, 1973

PAUL, W J, *and* ROBERTSON, K B. *Job enrichment and employee motivation*. London, Gower, 1970

PAYNE, Roy, *and* PUGH, Derek S. 'Organizational structure and climate', *in* Marvin D DUNNETTE (*ed*), *Handbook of industrial and organizational psychology*. Chicago, Rand McNally, 1976

PETERS, T J. *Thriving on chaos*. London, Pan, 1987

PFEFFER, Jeffrey. *Organizational design*. Arlington Heights, Ill., AHM, 1978

PLUNKETT, J J, and DALE, Barry G. 'Quality costing', in B G DALE and J J PLUNKETT (eds), *Managing quality*, Hemel Hempstead, Philip Allan, 1990

PORTER, LYMAN W, *and* LAWLER, Edward E. 'Properties of organizational structure in relation to job attitudes and job behavior', *Psychological Bulletin*, Vol 64, 1965, pp 23–51

PORTER, LYMAN W, *et al. Behavior in organizations*. New York, McGraw-Hill, 1975

PRICE, J L. *Handbook of organizational measurement*. Lexington, Mass., Heath, 1972

181

PUGH, D S, *and* HICKSON, David J. *Organizational structure and its context: the Aston programme 1.* Farnborough, Saxon House, 1976

REUTER, W. 'Procedures for participation in planning, developing and operating information systems', in P. DOHERTY *et al* (eds), *System design for human development and productivity: participation and beyond*, pp 345–58. Amsterdam, North-Holland, 1987.

ROBERTS, Karlene, *and* GLICK, William. 'The job characteristics approach to task design: a critical review', *Journal of Applied Psychology*, Vol 66, No 2, 1981, pp 193–217

ROBERTSON, Ivan T, *and* COOPER, Cary L. *Human behaviour in organisations.* Plymouth, Macdonald & Evans, 1983

ROETHLISBERGER, F J, *and* DICKSON, William J. *Management and the worker.* Cambridge, Mass., Harvard University Press, 1939

ROTTER, J B. 'Generalised expectancies for internal *v.* external control of reinforcement', *Psychological Monographs*, Vol 80, No 1, 1966, p. 609

ROUSSEAU, Denise M. 'Measures of technology as predictors of employee attitudes', *Journal of Applied Psychology*, Vol 63, No 2, 1978, pp 213–18

SALANCIK, G R, *and* PFEFFER, J. 'An examination of need-satisfaction models of job attitudes', *Administrative Science Quarterly*, Vol 22, No 3, 1977, pp 427–56

SCHEIN, Edgar H. *Organizational psychology*, 3rd edn. Englewood Cliffs, N.J., Prentice-Hall, 1980

SCHMIDT, Frank L, *et al.* 'Statistical power in criterion-related validation studies', *Journal of Applied Psychology*, Vol 61, No 4, 1976, pp 473–85

SEDDON, J. 'A passion for quality', *TQM Magazine*, May 1989, pp 153–7

SKINNER, B F. *About behaviorism.* New York, Knopf, 1974

SMITH, J M. 'Machine-paced work and stress', in C L COOPER and J M SMITH (eds), *Job stress in blue-collar work.* Chichester, Wiley, 1985

SMITH, J M, *and* ROBERTSON, I T. *The theory and practice of systematic staff selection.* London, Macmillan, 1986

SMITH, J M, *et al. Introducing organizational behavior.* London, Macmillan, 1982

SMITH, J M, *et al. British Telecom survey item bank*, Vol 1, *Measures of satisfaction.* Bradford, MCB, 1984

SMITH J M, *et al. British Telecom survey item bank*, Vol 2, *Measures of organization.* Bradford, MCB, 1984a

SMITH, J M, *et al. A development programme for women in management.* Aldershot, Gower, 1984b

SMITH, Patricia C, *et al. The measurement of satisfaction in work and retirement.* Chicago, Rand McNally, 1969

SMITH, Richard. *Introducing new technology into the office.* Work Research Unit Occasional paper 20. London, Work Research Unit, 1981

SMITH, Richard, *and* QUINLAN, Terry. 'Croydon Advertiser Group', *in* WORK RESEARCH UNIT, *Meeting the challenge of change: case studies.* London, WRU, 1982

SMITH, R B, *and* DUNHAM, F J. *Organizational surveys: an internal assessment of organizational health.* Glenview, Ill., Scott Foresman, 1979

SRIVASTA, Suresh *et al. Job satisfaction and productivity.* Cleveland, Case Western Reserve University, 1975

STAHL, M J. 'Achievement, power and managerial motivation: selecting managerial talent with the job choice exercise, *Personnel Psychology*, Vol 36, 1983, pp 775–89

STEERS, Richard M. 'Work environment and individual behavior', in Richard M STEERS and Lyman W PORTER (eds), *Motivation and work behavior*, 2nd edn. New York, McGraw-Hill, 1979

STEERS, Richard, *and* PORTER, Lyman W (eds), *Motivation and work behavior*, 2nd edn. New York, McGraw-Hill, 1979

SUTTON, Robert I, *and* ROUSSEAU, Denise M. 'Structure, technology and dependence on a parent organization: organizational and environmental correlates of individual responses', *Journal of Applied Psychology*, Vol 64, No 6, 1979, pp 675–87

TAKEZAWA, S, *et al. Improvements in quality of working life in three Japanese industries.* Geneva, International Labour Office, 1982

TAYLOR, Frederick Winslow. *The principles of scientific management.* New York, Harper, 1911

TAYLOR, James C. *Experiments in work system design: economic and human results.* Los Angeles, University of California Press, 1975

TAYLOR, James C. 'The human side of work: the socio-technical approach to work system design', *Personnel Review*, Vol 4, No 3, 1975a, pp 17–22

TAYLOR, M S, *et al.* 'Individuals' reactions to performance feedback in organizations: a control theory perspective', in K M ROWLAND and G R FERRIS (eds), *Research in personnel and human resources management*, Vol 2, 1984, pp 81–124

TERBORG, J R. 'Interactional psychology and research on human behavior in organizations', *Academy of Management Review*, Vol 4, 1981, pp 569–576

THOMPSON, James D. *Organizations in action.* New York, McGraw-Hill, 1967

TRIST, E L, *and* Bamforth, K W. 'Some social psychological consequences of the long wall method of coal getting', *Human Relations*, Vol 4, 1951, pp 1–38

TRIST, E L, *et al. Organizational choice: capabilities of groups at the coal face under changing technologies.* London, Tavistock, 1963

TSE, K K. 'Marks and Spencer: an anatomy of Britain's most efficiently managed company', Oxford, Pergamon 1985

TURNER, A N, *and* LAWRENCE, P R. *Industrial jobs and the worker: an investigation of response to task attributes.* Harvard University Graduate School of Business Administration, Boston, Mass., 1965

TYLER, T R, and BIES, R J. 'Beyond formal procedures: the interpersonal context of procedural justice', in J S CARROL (ed), *Applied social psychology and organizational settings*, pp 77–98. Hillsdale, N.J., Lawrence Earlbaum, 1990

UNITED STATES DEPARTMENT OF HEALTH EDUCATION AND WELFARE, *Work in America: report of a special task force* . . . Cambridge, Mass., MIT Press, 1973

VAN DER ZWANN, A H. 'The socio-technical systems approach: an evaluation', *International Journal of Production Engineering*, Vol. 13, 1975, pp 149–63

VEEN, P. 'Organization theories', in P J D DRENTH *et al.* (*eds*), *Handbook of work and organizational psychology.* Chichester, Wiley, 1984

VROOM, V. H. *Work and Motivation.* Chichester, Wiley, 1964

WAHBA, M A, *and* BRIDWELL, L G. 'Maslow reconsidered: a review of research on the need hierarchy theory', *in* Richard M STEERS *and* Lyman W PORTER (*eds*), *Motivation and work behavior*, 2nd edn. New York, McGraw-Hill, 1979

WALKER, Charles R, *and* GUEST, Robert H. *The man on the assembly line.* Cambridge, Mass., Harvard University Press, 1952

WALL, Toby D. 'Group work redesign in context: a two-phase model', *in* K D DUNCAN *et al.* (*eds*), *Changes in working life.* Chichester, Wiley, 1980

WALL, Toby D. 'What's new in job design?' *Personnel Management*, April 1984, pp 27–9

WALL, Toby D, *and* CLEGG, Chris W. 'A longitudinal field study of group work redesign', *Journal of Occupational Behaviour*, Vol 2, 1982, pp 31–49

WALL, Toby D, and DAVIDS, K. 'Shopfloor work organization and advanced manufacturing technology', in C L COOPER and I T ROBERTSON (eds), *International Review of Industrial and Organizational Psychology*, 1992

WALL, Toby D, and MARTIN, Robin. 'Job and work design', In C L COOPER and I T ROBERTSON (eds), *International Review of Industrial and Organizational Psychology*, 1987, pp 61–92

WALL, Toby D, *et al.* 'An evaluation of the job characteristics model', *Journal of Occupational Psychology*, Vol 51, No 2, 1978, pp 183–96

WALL, Toby D, *et al.* 'New technology, old jobs', *Work and People*, Vol 10, No 2, 1984

WALL, Toby D, *et al.* 'Advanced manufacturing technology, work design and performance: towards a theoretical framework', *Journal of Organizational Behaviour*, Vol 11, 1990, pp 201–19

WALL, Toby D, *et al.* 'Advanced manufacturing technology, work design and performance: a change study', *Journal of Applied Psychology*, Vol 75, 1990a.

WARR, Peter D. 'A national study of non-financial employment commitment', *Journal of Occupational Psychology*, Vol 55, No 4, 1982, pp 297–312

WARR, Peter. 'Psychological aspects of employment and unemployment', *Psychological Medicine*, Vol 12, 1982a, pp 7–11

WEBER, Max. *The theory of social and economic organization*, rev. edn, trans. A M HENDERSON and T PARSONS. London, Oxford University Press, 1947

WEED, Earl D. 'Job enrichment "cleans up" at Texas Instruments', in John R MAHER (ed), *New perspectives in job enrichment*. New York, Van Nostrand Reinhold, 1971

WEICK, Karl E. *The social psychology of organizing*, 2nd edn. Reading, Mass., Addison-Wesley, 1979

WEISS, H M, and RAKESTRAW, T L. 'Effects of social influences and task experience on goals, expectancies for goal attainment, and performance level attractiveness', unpublished manuscript, Department of Psychological Sciences, Purdue University, 1988

WHITE, G C. *Job design and individual differences*. Work Research Unit. Occasional Paper 9. London, Work Research Unit, 1977

WHITE, G C. *Redesign of work organizations: its impact on supervisors*. Work Research Unit Occasional Paper 26. London, Work Research Unit, 1983

WILKINSON, Adrian. 'The other side of quality: 'soft' issues and the human resource dimension', *Total Quality Management Journal*, 1992

WILKINSON, Adrian, and WITCHER, Barry. 'Fitness for use? Barriers to full TQM in the UK', 5th annual conference, British Academy of Management, 1991

WILKINSON, Adrian, *et al.* 'TQM and the management of labour', *Employee Relations*, Vol 13, 1991, pp 24–31

WILSON, John R. 'Participation: a framework and a foundation for ergonomics', *Journal of Occupational Psychology*, Vol 64, 1991, pp 67–80

WILSON, John R, and GREY, S M. 'Perceived characteristics of the work environment', in O BROWN and H HENDRICKS eds), *Human Factors in Organizational Design and Management*, Vol. II. Amsterdam, Elsevier, 1986

WOLK, S, *and* KURTZ, J. 'Positive adjustment and involvement during ageing and expectancy for internal control', *Journal of Consulting and Clinical Psychology*, Vol 43, 1975, pp 173–8

WOOD, S (ed). *The transformation of work?* London, Unwin Hyman, 1989

WOODWARD, Joan. *Management and technology*. London, HMSO, 1958

WOODWARD, Joan. *Industrial organization: theory and practice*. London, Oxford University Press, 1965

WORK RESEARCH UNIT. *Meeting the challenge of change: case studies*. London, WRU, 1982

WORK RESEARCH UNIT. *Report of the Tripartite Steering Group on Job Satisfaction*. London, WRU, 1983

WYATT, S, *et al. The comparative effects of variety and uniformity in work*. Medical Research Council, Industrial Fatigue Research Board, Report 52. London, HMSO, 1928

ZOCCARO, S J, and STONE, E F. 'Incremental validity of an empirically based measure of job characteristics', *Journal of Applied Psychology*, Vol 73, 1988, pp 245–52

184

Author index

Ackoff R 7, 9
Adams J S 48
Alderfer C P 25
Algera J A 65–6, 158
Alschuler A S 166
Andrews J D W 149
Annett J 52
Argyris C 18
Arnold H J 65
Arvey R D 35
Ashford S J 48, 158
Atkinson P E 147
Austin J T 41
Avergold M 121

Babchuck N 157
Bagchus P M 17
Bamforth K W 123
Bandura A 31, 36, 43, 48, 146, 150, 167
Bedeian A G 11
Bendix R 3
Bies R J 40, 49
Blackler F H M 134–5
Blandy A 125
Blau P M 17, 157
Blauner R 60
Blum M L 53, 54
Boaden R J 154
Bobko P 41
Boddy D 124, 126
Boje D M 18
Botterill M 147, 158
Bowers D G 86, 100
Boyatzis R E 144
Brand D D 35
Bridwell L G 24
Bright K 146, 148
Brown C A 134–5

Bryan J F 38
Buchanan D A 124, 126
Burns T 11, 12, 154
Butteriss M 121

Cameron S 100
Campbell D J 69
Campbell J P 13
Campion M A 47, 71
Caplan R D 150
Carby K 111, 113
Carver C S 47
Cattell R B 164
Central Statistical Office 116
Cervone D 48
Champoux J E 65, 66
Child D 164
Child J 148, 156
Clegg C W 58, 128–30
Cochran W C 91
Collard R 145, 151
Cook J D 92
Cooper C L 37
Cooper M D 40
Cooper R 58–64, 103, 105, 112, 134
Crosby P B 144
Cross D 94
Cummings L L 158
Cyert R 13

Dale B G 146, 147, 148
Davids K 194, 105
Davis L E 5, 69, 125
Davis S M 155
Davis T R V 31
Deming W E 145
Dickinson A M 31, 36
Dickson W J 3
Dipboye R L 165

Dowrick P W 44, 167
Dubin R 104
Dumas R A 147
Dunham P J 86, 88–9, 100

Eder R W 165
Ellul J 2
Emery F E 7, 9, 69, 131, 146
Erez M 28, 40, 41
European Commission Resolution 121 565

Feigenbaum A V 145
Fein M 118, 132, 134
Ferris G R 66, 68, 165
Fine S A 52
Fineman S 144
Ford R N 62, 111, 122–3, 150
Franklin J L 100
Frayne C A 167, 168
Fraser J A 59
French J R P 150
Fried Y 66, 68
Frost P J 104

Galbraith J R 155
Garland H 43
Garvin D A 158
Gerhart B 69
Glick W 65, 66
Goode W J 157
Gough H G 144
Gouldner A W 4
Gray J 35
Greenberg J 48, 49
Greenroos C 145
Grey S M 153
Guest R H 59
Gulick L H 3, 16
Gulowsen J 70
Gyllenhammer P G 126–8

Hackman J R 11, 52, 62–3, 65, 67, 68, 72–5, 82, 95, 102, 111, 116, 134–5, 150, 160–1
Hall D T 22–4
Hamner E P 36
Hamner W C 36
Handy C B 10, 11, 154
Hellriegal D 148

Hendrick C F 159
Hengen W K 108, 111, 112
Herold D M 158
Herzberg F 56–8, 102, 111, 116
Hickson D J 10
Hill S 145, 148, 149, 152, 154
Hollenbeck J R 151
Hood M 44, 167
House R J 65
Hunter J E 66

Ilgen D R 44
Imada A S 151
Indik B P 151
Ishikawa K 156
Ivancevich J M 35

James L R 10, 14
Jones A P 10, 14
Juan J M 145, 146

Kahn R L 7, 158
Kalton G 91
Kanfer F H 167
Kanfer R 151
Karoly P 169
Katz D 7, 158
Kazdin A E 35
Kemp N J 71, 131, 135
Kernon M C 48
Kiggundu M N 65
Klein H J 47, 48
Klein L 71
Kline P 164
Kotter J P 15
Kreitner R 31, 34, 35, 36
Krejcie R V 90
Kurtz J 139

Lascelles D M 147, 158
Latham G P 39, 40, 41, 48, 167, 168
Lawler E E 17, 26, 29, 37, 62–3, 88, 143
Lawrence P R 11, 12, 58–60, 62, 63, 102, 154, 155
Leavitt H J 18
Levitt T 158
Lewin K 108, 109, 110
Likert R 88
Locke E A 35, 38, 39, 41, 43–4, 118,

120, 122, 134, 160
Lord R G 47, 48
Lorsch J W 11, 12, 13, 154
Lupton T 51
Luthans F 31, 34, 35, 36

Mahoney T A 104
Mambrey P 150
Mansfield R 11
March J G 13
Maslow A H 20–6, 56, 116, 143
Mayo E 3
McClelland D C 144, 162–3
McGregor D 13, 159
Merton R K 4
Miller G A 47
Mirvis P H 88
Morgan O W 90
Moser C A 91

Nadler D A 29, 37, 158
Naylor J C 40, 53, 54
Nemeroff W F 40, 170, 172
Nie N H 97, 99
Nougaim K E 22–4
Nuttin J 48

Oakland J 145, 146, 147, 151, 159
O'Brien R M 31, 36
Oldham G R 11, 63, 65, 67, 68, 82,
    95, 102, 111, 116, 150, 160–1
Orpen C 132–3
O'Toole J 121

Parsons C K 158
Paul W J 106, 123
Payne R 11, 13
Peters T J 145
Pfeffer J 12, 66
Plunkett J J 146, 148
Pondy L R 18
Porter L W 26, 28, 143, 156, 163
Price J L 92
Pugh D S 10, 11, 13

Quinlan T 124

Rakestraw T L 44
Reuter W 151
Rhode J G 17

Roberts K 65, 66
Robertson I T 37, 52, 53, 54
Robertson K B 106, 123
Robertson M M 151
Roethlisberger F J 3
Rosow M P 31, 36
Rotter J B 162
Rousseau D M 14

Salancik G R 66
Scheier M F 47
Schein E H 18, 155
Schmidt F L 94
Seddon J 159
Sirota D 134
Skinner B F 31
Smith J M 52, 53, 54, 86, 88–9, 92,
    100, 148, 167
Smith P C 94, 97
Smith R 124, 125, 143
Srivasta S 134
Stahl M J 144
Stalker G M 11, 12, 154
Stepina L P 82
Steers R M 28, 75, 76, 163
Stock F G L 59
Stone E F 69
Sutton R I 14

Takezawa S 121
Tanner I 51
Taylor F W 2–3, 104
Taylor J C 69, 123, 125
Taylor M S 41
Terborg J R 22
Thayer P W 71
Thompson J D 104
Triplett A 159
Trist E L 6, 123
Tse K K 155
Turner A N 58–60, 62, 63, 102
Tyler T R 40, 49

Urwick L 3
U.S. Department of Health,
    Education and Welfare 116
University of Manchester Institute
    of Science and Technology,
    Manchester School of
    Management 139

Van Der Zwann A H 71
Van Dooren F J P 17
Veen P 3, 4
Vroom V H 158

Wahba M A 24
Walker C R 59, 104, 105
Wall T D 65, 67, 75, 126, 128–30, 146
Warr P B 1
Weber M 3, 4
Weed E D 117
Weick K E 16
Weiss H M 44
Wexley K N 40, 170

White G C 126, 1£35
Wiley W W 52
Wilkinson A 145, 152, 153, 159
Wilson J R 150, 153, 154
Witcher B 152, 153
Wolfson A D 134
Wolk S 139
Wood S 67
Woodward J 11, 12, 103
Work Research Unit 122–4
Wyatt S 59

Zidon I 40
Zoccaro S J 69

Subject index

AWG *see* Autonomous Work
  Groups
Absenteeism 7–8, 33, 60, 62, 88,
  134, 138, 151
Achievement motivation 143–4,
  165–9
Activation 39
Age
  and motivation 85, 138–40
American Telephone and Telegraph
  Company 22, 118, 122
Analysis of production techniques
  159
Anxiety 108
Appraisal
  in motivation 168–71
Authority figure 40, 47
Autonomous Work Groups 69–70,
  72, 73, 106–7, 127–34, 153, 154,
  156
Autonomy 64, 67, 73, 103, 129–30,
  143, 153, 156, 160

Behaviour
  conditioning 30
  modification 22, 31, 155
  theories 30–8
Bell Telephone System 62
Build-up feedback 100
Bureaucracy
  system 12, 17
  theory 3–4

CPI *see* California Psychological
  Inventory
California Psychological Inventory
  144
Cascade strategy *see* Waterfall
  strategy

Change
  implementation 114–5
  job redesign 121–36
  models 111–5
Coacting groups 74–5
Communication 154–5
  and surveys 80, 85–6
  distrust 74
Competition 7, 156
Congruence 12, 17
Content
  theory 20–6
Contingency theory 12
Continuous learning 71
Contributions 61–2
Control systems
  and motivation 157–60
  theory 47–8 (*see* Self-regulation)
Critical behaviour 34

Data handback 87
Disincentive 40
Discretion
  in work 60
Deeks & Co. 82
Determinism 12
Development groups 109, 113
Dissatisfiers *see* Hygiene factors

Employees 157, 172
  and appraisal 168–71
  and organizations 17
  attitudes to change 38, 105–6,
    147–8
  motivation surveyed 86–7, 131–4,
    162
  rewards for performance 29–34,
    38–44
  selection 164–5
  variety in work 106–7

Environment
  and motivation 151–5
  effect on behaviour 21–2, 75,
    117–8
  of organization 15
Equity 40, 48–9, 74, 153
Ergs 163
Expectancies 41–4 (see Subjective
  probability of success)
Expectancy theory 25–30, 37, 41, 43
Expectancy-valence theory 27–30,
  37, 43, 166–69
Externals 162
Extinction 33, 35
Extrinsic satisfiers 93

Fair play see Equity
Feedback 47, 58, 160
  and performance 36, 39, 40, 41,
    62–4, 73, 101, 129–30, 170
  from surveys 87–8, 101–2

GNS see Growth need strength
Goals
  and performance 38–43, 62
  setting 38–41, 110, 122–3, 131,
    168–70
Growth need strength 64, 66, 143,
  160

HUD see Dept. of Housing and
  Urban Development
Hanover Radio Company 88
Hawthorne effect 117
Human relations
  theory 4
Human resource accounting 88
Human resource management 159
Hygiene factors 56

ICI 106, 123
Identity 129–30
Individuals 138, 145, 146
  and job design 160
  development of 66, 86–7, 150, 162
  exclusion of 138, 153
Industrial Fatigue Research Board
  59
Instrumentality 2–3, 27–8
Interest tests 164–5

Internal market 151–2
Internals 162
Interpersonal process consultation
  87
Intrinsic satisfiers 93

JCE see Job Choice Exercise
JDI see Job Descriptive Index
JDS see Job Diagnostic Survey
Job
  and motivation 56, 157–60
  see also Tasks, Work
Job analysis 52, 54–5
Job characteristics 62–7, 70–1, 130,
  132, 136, 160
Job Choice Exercise 144
Job context characteristics 72–7
Job description 53–4
  surveys 84
Job Descriptive Index 94, 97, 99
Job design 51, 79–83, 102–20, 161
  and motivation 157–60
  employee attitudes 105, 128
  evaluation 114–20
  experiments 123, 128–36
  greenfield sites 131
  management attitudes 105
  planned change 107–15
  redesign 107, 116–20, 129–32, 134
  technology 103–5, 108, 123–7
  union attitudes 105
  see also Motivation
Job Diagnostic Survey 67–9, 82–3,
  95, 129, 133
Job enlargement 72, 106–7, 110,
  122–3
Job enrichment 72, 106–7, 110,
  119–20
  and job redesign 116–8, 129, 133
Job rotation 72, 106, 128
Job satisfaction 51, 56–7, 76–7, 80–
  2, 88, 123, 134, 136, 138–44
Job security
  satisfaction with 79
'Just-in-Time' inventory control
  158

Kuder Vocational Interest Test 164

Laboratory training 87

190

MAT *see* Motivational Analysis
  Test
Mp *see* Managerial potential
MPS *see* Motivation Potential Score
Management attitudes 105, 147–8
Management effectiveness 87
Managerial potential 144
Managers
  as motivators 29–30, 143
  dissatisfaction with 81
  job satisfaction 143–5
Manchester School of Management
  (UMIST) 139–40
Marks and Spencer's engineering
  department 155
Matrix (design/structure) 154/5
McGregor's (1960) Concept of
  Theory X and Theory Y 159
Meaningfulness
  of work 63
Measuring motivation in employees
  162–4
Miners 6–7
Minimum cost 3
Money *see* Remuneration
Morale 78, 89, 166
  raising 165
Motivating Potential Score 68
Motivation 2, 137–44
  and behaviour 30–8
  and job design 5, 62, 76
  and management 29–30, 143–4,
    167
  and organizations 1, 29–30, 75,
    78–101, 149, 157
  and performance 29–30, 35–6, 38,
    62, 131, 137, 159
  and redundancy 165
  and work characteristics 51–77
  case studies 78–83, 116
  content theory of 20–5
  expectancy-valence theory of
    27–30, 37
  individual 138
  measuring 83–4, 89–90, 92
  process theory of 25–9
  tested 164–5
  theories 44
Motivational Analysis Test 163, 164
Motivator-hygiene theory *see* Two

factor theory
Motivators
  surveyed 93

Nach *see* Achievement motivation
Need hierarchy
  theory 20–6
  tests 22–3
Negative reinforcement 33
New technology
  impact of 6–7, 11, 123–6

OB *see* Organizations, behaviour in
OD *see* Organization development
Occupation
  differences in motivation 140–4
  groups 140, 142–4
Open systems
  theory 7–8, 15
Operant conditioning 32, 34, 37
Organization development
  surveys 85–8
Organizational behaviour
  modification 16, 31–8, 44
Organizational characteristics
  measures of 95
Organizational climate 13–15, 75–6
  161
Organizational effectiveness 13
Organizational system 15–6
Organizations
  and congruence 12, 18
  and job design 161
  and people 16–7
  behaviour in 31–41
  context of 95
  functions of 16
  medium sized 81–2
  models of 8–9
  motivation in 78–101, 153
  multinational 79–81
  open systems 8
  ostrich 108
  process 96
  small 82–3
  structure 9–13, 95, 151–7
  technology 11–13
  theories 3–9, 17
  values 96
Ostrich strategy 108

191

PSE *see* Picture Story Exercises
Participation 40–3, 110, 113, 149,
    165–8
    in surveys 89–91
Pay *see* Remuneration
Peer group influence 40
Performance
    and feedback 35–6, 122–3
    and motivation 26, 29–30, 35–6,
        62, 88, 130, 137–44
    behavioural approach 31–2
    measure 45
Picture Story Exercises 162–3
Positive reinforcement 32–3, 35
Process
    theories 25
Productivity 8, 134
    and motivation 38, 137–8
Programmed jobs 103
Promotion 26, 79, 139
Psychological climate 14
Psychological models
    of motivation 19–44, 62–9
    of organizations 14, 17–8
Punishment 33, 35

Quality *see* Total Quality
    Management
Quality of working life 102, 120–3
Questionnaires 66, 71–7
    to measure motivation 79
    see also Surveys

Race
    differences in motivation 149
Reciprocal determinism 37
Redundancy
    motivation 165
Reinforcement *see* Rewards
Remuneration
    as motivating factor 1, 79, 110,
        130–1, 171–2
Rewards
    by race 149
    in job characteristics model 63–4
    linked to performance 29, 32,
        169–70, 171
    organizational implication 30
    see also Remuneration

Rothwell Miller Test 164
Rotter's (1960) Scale of the Locus of
    Control 162

SPS *see* Subjective Probability of
    Success (*also* Expectancies)
SPSS *see* Statistical Package for the
    Social Sciences
Safety needs 20, 22–3, 40
Satisfiers 56, 93
Scales
    calculation 97–100
    for measuring motivation 92–5
Scientific administration
    theory 4
Scientific management 2–4
Selection
    of motivated staff 164–5
Self-actualization 20–4
Self-efficacy 39, 41–4, 167–8, 169
Self-regulation 47–8 (*see also*
    Control theory)
Sentiments 163
Sex
    differences in motivation 140–1
Simultaneous feedback 100
Skill discretion 60
Skill variety 64, 73, 103–4
Social learning theory 36–8, 44
Socio-technical systems
    in coal mines 6–8
    theory 5–7, 69–72
    see also Tavistock Institute
Statistical Package for the Social
    Sciences 97
Statistics
    descriptive statistics 97–100
Strong Vocational Interest
    Inventory 164
Subjective probability of success
    41–4 (*see also* Expectancies)
Suffolk Area Ambulance Service
    125
Surveys
    analysis 97–100
    diagnostic 84, 88
    financial benefit 88–89
    for organizational development
        85–88
    investigative 85

preparation 89–91
questionnaires 91–7
results 100–1
sampling fraction 91
to measure job satisfaction 79–82

TAT *see* Thematic Apperception Test
TOTE *see* Test Operate, Test Exit
TQM *see* Total Quality Management
T Group training 87
Task and process consultation 87
Task identity 62–3, 73
Task significance 64, 73
Tasks 52, 62, 72–3
   and job design 73–7
   and motivation 56–9, 69
   see also Work
Tavistock Institute 5–9
Team development training 87
Technological change
   in job design 103–4, 108, 123–7
   see also New technology
Test Operate, Test Exit 47
Texas Instruments (TI) 118
Thematic Apperception test 144, 162, 164
Total Quality Management 137, 145–64
Training 137, 165–8
   satisfaction with 79, 81–2, 85–7
Turnover

of employees 81–2, 85, 88, 134, 138, 151
Two factor theory 56–8, 117
Typists
   impact of work processing 124

United States, Department of Housing and Urban Development (HUD) 35–6

Valence 28–9
Validity
   of questionnaires 94–5
Variance 66
Variety 102
   and boredom 59
Volvo 107, 127–8, 131–2

Waterfall strategy
   for feedback 100–1
Women
   motivation 138, 140–1, 167
Work
   and motivation 51–77, 129
   behaviour 19–50
   benefits 1
   characteristics 51–77
   discretion in 60
   performance 2, 63, 77
Work groups *see* Autonomous Work Groups
Work teams 73–5